T0243933

PRAISE FOR *SHY BY DESIGN*

"In *Shy by Design*, Michael Thompson provides a transformative guide for introverts. Thompson's wisdom on building meaningful connections and amplifying personal impact is game-changing. A must-read for those who feel their quiet nature is a disadvantage."—**Darius Foroux**, author of eight books, including *Do It Today* and *The Stoic Path to Wealth*

"Thompson is a master at profound simplicity. He lays down his words with such grace and economy that while reading *Shy by Design*, I found myself frequently pausing because he expressed a human truth that hit something deep inside me. This is one of those precious books that deserves a coveted place on your nightstand to guide you throughout your life and career.—**Kevin Kelley**, co-founder of Shook Kelley and author of *Irreplaceable*

"Engaging and actionable. Thompson's journey is very inspiring and the lessons he's learned about owning our story and building the right relationships are things we can all implement. If you're looking to live with more authenticity and purpose, read *Shy by Design*."—**Kim Dabbs**, Global VP of ESG + Social Innovation at Steelcase and bestselling author of *You Belong* Here

"Uplifting and highly actionable, *Shy by Design* shows us that we don't need to be the loudest person in the room to influence others in meaningful ways.'—**Michelle Woo**, award-winning journalist and former senior editor at Medium.com

"Among the myriad tales of individuals overcoming personal struggles, none provide the refreshing clarity and unconventional actionable steps found in this narrative. Within a few hours of reading *Shy by Design*, I took Thompson's unique insights to connect authentically, which not only led to personal growth but also a positive impact on others."—**Benjamin Sledge**, combat-wounded veteran and award-winning author of *Where Cowards Go to* Die

"*Shy by Design*" cuts through the noise in our increasingly loud world and provides an action-driven roadmap to living life on our own terms. Thompson's story will stay with you for years to come while serving as a source of inspiration to summon the courage to bet on yourself."—**Brian Pennie**, PhD, award-winning author of *Bonus Time*, recovering heroin addict turned neuroscientist, and motivational speaker

SHY BY DESIGN

SHY BY DESIGN

12 Timeless Principles to Quietly Stand Out

MICHAEL THOMPSON

ROWMAN & LITTLEFIELD
Lanham • Boulder • New York • London

Published by Rowman & Littlefield
An imprint of The Rowman & Littlefield Publishing Group, Inc.
4501 Forbes Boulevard, Suite 200, Lanham, Maryland 20706
www.rowman.com

86-90 Paul Street, London EC2A 4NE

Distributed by NATIONAL BOOK NETWORK

Library of Congress Cataloging-in-Publication Data

Names: Thompson, Michael, 1978- author.
Title: Shy by design : 12 timeless principles to quietly stand out / Michael Thompson.
Description: Lanham : Rowman & Littlefield, [2024] | Includes bibliographical
   references and index. | Summary: "This book shares the transformation from feeling
   left out to leading others while staying true to his shy nature. Through simple
   frameworks, flips on conventional wisdom, and inspiring human experience stories,
   readers will be armed with the communication skills to own their voice, build win-win
   relationships, and grow their influence through the power of words. In addition to
   the principles, readers will be equipped with resource banks consisting of phrases of
   exactly what to say - and what not to say - in various situations to drive their personal
   relationships and professional opportunities forward"-- Provided by publisher.
Identifiers: LCCN 2024003465 | ISBN 9781538175842 (cloth) | ISBN 9781538175859
   (epub)
Subjects: LCSH: Introversion. | Interpersonal communication. | Leadership.
Classification: LCC BF698.35.I59 T466 2024 | DDC 658.4/092--dc23/eng/20240415
LC record available at https://lccn.loc.gov/2024003465

To Luc and Liam, never stop using your "brains for thinking"
and drawing giraffes without necks.

CONTENTS

Start Here xi

Part I: Persistently Curious 1
Principle 1: Embrace Your Imperfections 3
Principle 2: Lead with Listening. 19
Principle 3: Treat Your Curiosity as Your Primary
Responsibility 31
Principle 4: Grow Your Confidence in Private. 45
Part II: Meaningful Connections 59
Principle 5: Get to Know Your Heroes 61
Principle 6: Friendships Are Forged in the Follow-Up 79
Principle 7: Small Is the New Big 95
Principle 8: Gain New Eyes through the Power of Weak
Ties. 109
Part III: Quiet Conviction 121
Principle 9: Share What You're Learning 123
Principle 10: Own Your Story 137
Principle 11: Be Bold in the Moments That Matter. 151
Principle 12: Lift as You Climb 167
The Final Word 179

Contents

Acknowledgments 181

Notes 183

Bibliography 187

Index 189

About the Author 203

Start Here

When my son Liam finished first grade, my wife, Laia, and I sat down with his teacher for his year-end review. She explained that during the last week of each school year, she asks the students to write the name of the one classmate they appreciated most having by their side. Given that Liam is shy and has a speech impediment, we were surprised to learn that he and the other reserved children dominated the list. "It's like this every year," his teacher told us as she showed us the nice comments his classmates had written about him. "It's always the quiet ones. It really makes you question who the truly popular kids are, doesn't it?"

Growing up, I allowed my shyness, severe stutter, and crippling social anxiety to dominate my internal dialog and undermine my hopes and dreams. Not only did some of my peers mock me, but even a few of my teachers joined in, further reinforcing the self-limiting belief that I was better off tucked away in a corner safe from harm's way.

Shortly after graduating college, though, out of fear of never mustering the courage to step into my voice, I chose to pursue the one job that scared me the most: sales.

I got into the field thinking the short-term pain of looking like a fool would help me feel like less of one in the long run. Looking back, I succeeded on both accounts. People hung up on me. Some of my coworkers made fun of me. Despite the heckling, something profound happened the longer I kept my head down and blocked the noise. I excelled.

But this wasn't because I tried to be like the confident and charismatic people in the office. I realized I'd never win if I played their game, so I invented my own. With time, my eyes opened to two revelations: there's beauty in our "perceived" weaknesses, and fulfillment is found in doing what we can—with what we have—to help other people succeed.

Though "simple," these shifts changed everything. By the end of my first calendar year, after getting clear on my initial set of personal operating principles, I broke into the top ten of the company-wide salesforce before being promoted to management where I led a high-producing team and trained all new hires.

My career in coaching, communication, and entrepreneurship has since taken me into classrooms and boardrooms across the globe. I've worked in traditional leadership roles in corporate America and I've learned firsthand what it's like to lose it all while pursuing entrepreneurial endeavors in Central America. Today, from a small coastal town outside of Barcelona, Spain, I teach leadership and communication skills to students pursuing their master's, serve as a communication advisor, write for mainstream business and life publications, and help seasoned executives and entrepreneurs share their stories and grow their influence.

In short, some people focus on their strengths to win the life they want. I didn't. I chose to pursue the opposite path. For the first twenty-three years of my life, I was so paralyzed by my supposed afflictions that I was too scared and embarrassed to even try to identify any potential strengths. By choosing to put myself out into the world and making a commitment to collect blisters instead of chasing bliss, I stepped into the person I didn't even know I was capable of becoming.

But the purpose of this book isn't to convince you to pursue sales like I did. Quite the contrary. Packaged in twelve easy-to-grasp principles and broken down into three parts, this book chronicles my transformation from feeling left out to leading others while staying true to my shy and quiet nature. Although the principles serve as my north star for how I want to show up in the world, the primary goal of this book is to help you cement your own principles that are authentic to you and your way of being.

Part I, "Persistently Curious," kicks off with the eye-opening lessons I learned during the onset of my experience in sales that helped me view myself through a more empowered lens. We'll explore actionable ways to slowly expand our comfort zone in social situations as well as lay the foundation to master the art of conversation, which I define as creating the space for people to reveal themselves. When we lead with listening, treat our curiosity as our primary responsibility, and commit to the foundational behind-the-scenes work to more confidently express ourselves, the doors open to identify how our story and those of the people around us can best collide.

Part II, "Meaningful Connections," is brimming with proven suggestions and systems to create a supportive network that advances our careers and adds more meaning to our lives. There is no "hack" more effective than optimizing for quality relationships. If we surround ourselves with the right people, life is not only more fun but the challenges we face become less daunting. In addition to exploring ways to connect with people we admire and nurturing those budding friendships through thoughtful follow-ups, we'll dive into the power that lies in keeping our world small and the surprising strength of "weak tie" relationships.

Last, in Part III, "Quiet Conviction," we'll uncover our voices and scale the impact we want to make in the world. By committing to share what we're learning and taking the steps to own our story, we build our boldness muscle to move forward in the moments that matter, even when feeling shaky. I'm proud that I've faced my fears and obstacles my way. But I never would have had the courage to pursue my goals if it hadn't been for the support of so many people who saw potential in me when I couldn't see it for myself. The final principle, "Lift as You Climb," is rooted in the most effective way to grow our confidence: choose to be the type of person who builds the confidence of others.

While I'm still shy, and at times I still stutter, I wouldn't want it any other way. If there's one thing I've learned in life, it's that being underestimated is a superpower, and the only freedom that truly matters is waking up each day with the courage to be yourself.

For the better part of my life, I didn't think I had a story, and I sure didn't think people would care about what I had to say. But I was wrong. We don't need to be overly outgoing to make a difference in the lives of the people we care about, and we certainly don't need to be society's definition of an influencer to be influential.

The world is moving quickly. It's also become incredibly loud. Instead of joining in on the noise, I hope the inspiring stories and actionable frameworks within the pages that follow encourage you to continue listening to yourself and others while providing you with strategies to better bet on yourself.

We all have a story.

The world needs to hear yours.

Part I

Persistently Curious

Principle 1

Embrace Your Imperfections

"What am I doing here?" I thought to myself. "This isn't for me. I'm way out of my element."

Cigarette packs, coffee cups, and manilla folders littered the desks. I felt like I'd just walked onto the set of a bad sales movie. The year was 2003. The place was an old furniture warehouse turned into a bustling mortgage company in downtown Baltimore. My head was spinning. The sales reps who weren't screaming into their phones were yelling at each other about how many deals they had going. But just as I began to plot my escape to join my unemployed roommates on the couch, the corporate trainer stuck his head outside the conference room door and shouted, "We're in here, Mike! Let's go!"

I walked into the room, my palms dripping with sweat. All the information thrown at me and the other trainees over the next couple of hours didn't help to calm my nerves. But in between the sales talk and industry lingo I pretended to understand, the trainer said something I could get my head around: "If you make one hundred calls a day, I don't care who you are, you'll make 100K!"

Upon hearing this, the other newbies in the room were stoked. Even though I'm usually cautious of big promises from a fast-talking guy in a suit and tie, something clicked. But this wasn't just because I saw flashes of retirement; it was also because

I knew if I sucked it up for a few months, I'd get better at building connections with people, which as a shy person with a severe stutter was a skill I was desperate to improve. I needed to do something—anything—to get more comfortable around people to limit the number of internal panic attacks I had every time someone called my name. Getting in front of as many people as possible as fast as possible seemed like the best way to overcome my fears. Plus, the phone was better than in person. I could hold a stress ball. My left leg could twitch as much as it wanted. I could even blame the connection if things went south, which they did—a lot.

The next day, I walked into the office, ready to go. But my good mood immediately got flipped upside-down when the corporate trainer said two words that most sane people dread: "Role plays!"

"Role plays" can be fun in certain situations. But nine times out of ten, those instances take place outside office walls. If you aren't familiar with the term, you aren't missing much. You and a partner or two act out your sales call to tighten your pitch before presenting it to the entire group.

I was paralyzed for a solid minute. Once the fog began to lift from my nightmare reality, I heard my name being shouted from across the training floor. After figuring out how to use my legs again, I stumbled over to my newly appointed manager in a state of pure panic. The fact he was pushing six-foot-five and had a reputation for being as charismatic as Bill Clinton didn't help me walk any straighter.

"You don't look too good," he said. "What's up?"

I wanted to play it cool, but I didn't. "I stutter and I took this job to . . ." were the only words I managed to muster before his catcher-mitt-sized hand swallowed my shoulder.

"What do you want to do?"

"Not role plays!" I replied in a rare moment of clarity and conviction.

"Hmmm. I have an idea. Come with me."

Rather than explain the situation to the corporate trainer on the way out, he simply told him he was stealing me for the day. "I hate that shit, too," he said to my surprise while walking toward my desk. "Here's a pile of dead leads and a few scripts. Make your way through them and let me know if you get hung up on anything."

"You're not going to sit with me?" I asked.

"The fact you had the guts to show up tells me you'll do just fine. Plus, most people don't last long if they don't wanna come to work. Try to get comfortable. I'll be in my office if you need anything."

I liked my manager. He took it fast and loud with some and slow and quiet with others. By reading the room and treating people as individuals, he created a culture where the masses followed him.

For the next few months, I did my job and picked up the phone. Again. And again. And again. Making not only 100 calls a day but 110. This wasn't because I wanted a new Escalade or even a used one. It was because, on 10 percent of the calls, I stuttered so badly when introducing myself, I hung up the phone.

To this day, I still struggle to say words that start with the letter "m." Considering my name is "M-M-Michael" and my job was selling "m-m-mortgages," I delivered some of the worst (and lengthiest) pitches in the history of sales. Despite this, in between silently blasting my parents for giving me this "boy named Sue" curse, and thinking about the legal ramifications of referring to myself as Todd or Bob, a few interesting things happened over the following months that made me panic much less.

RETHINK THE WORLD ORDER

The "success" advice dominating markets reads like played-out tropes: "Act more confident!" "Crush your comfort zone!" "Stand like an Alpha!" It's hard not to buy into this narrative; it's rammed down our throats. Everywhere we turn, we're reminded that the truly strong crush things.

But true to the corporate trainer's words, three months into the job I witnessed firsthand that he was dead right in his promise. Introverts. Extroverts. White. Black. Single moms. Recent college grads. Charismatic. Quiet. It didn't matter. The people with the highest number of calls were the very names announced as the company's sales leaders at the year-end holiday party. To my surprise, the top salesperson was shy and introverted. Some of my coworkers considered him socially awkward. But he knew something I hadn't yet internalized: the world is full of people who prefer those who lead with care instead of worrying about demonstrating bullet-proof confidence. By showing up, prioritizing his client's interests over his own, and leaning into his own unique strengths, he stood out.

Realizing that hard work was the great equalizer and that my shyness wasn't a factor was inspiring to witness. The actions of the sales leaders in the office, and others who did good work, helped to slowly flip my self-talk from feeling worthless to worthwhile.

Around the same time that my eyes were opened to the fact that reserved, quiet, or shy people could not only compete in sales but win, our team had to attend a sales seminar. Initially, I wasn't very excited about having to go to the event. To this day, I much prefer intimate settings over large crowds. But I'm sure glad I went to the seminar because the keynote speaker said something that shook my world.

I wish I could remember his name. He was a big deal. Much like how some people today admire Elon Musk, when the man came out onto the stage, the audience went nuts. The applause he garnered was well deserved for sure. But it was a throwaway line toward the end of his talk that made both me and my team erupt. "Oh, one last thing," he said nonchalantly while gathering up his stuff. "If you're having trouble getting people to talk—stutter. They'll see you as a human being instead of a salesperson!"

"WW-W-W-What?" I said to myself. "Holy Shit-t-tt-t-tt!" I then yelled to myself, "I can stutter! I know how to stutter! I don't even have to fake it till I m-m-make it!"

Shortly after, many of my clients expressed how much they respected and appreciated me going into sales. "You're not like other salespeople," they told me. "It's a refreshing change. You got guts. I feel like you're actually listening to me and you're not some fast-talker trying to snowball me!"

All those years of beating myself up, and it turns out my unique selling point was being myself. My mind was blown. Sure, I wasn't for everyone. But I didn't have to be. Twelve months later, I was presented with an award for being the ninth top-producing salesperson in the company at our year-end holiday party before being promoted to the management team.

If you think about this progression, it makes perfect sense. When you cut through the noise, people want to spend time and work with individuals they like and trust. I couldn't smooth-talk my way out of jams, so I did my best not to put myself in any. I leaned into my slowly rising strengths of listening, putting myself in the client's shoes, wanting the best for them, and thinking of creative and beneficial ways to help solve their problems. Not worrying so much about demonstrating bullet-proof confidence but choosing the route of comfort, reliability, and kindness changed everything.

The beauty of this strategy is it can net the same results as being more outgoing, but it has the potential to make you stress a lot less. The key, however, is found in how you choose to define the word "confidence." For me, and many of the people I've spent time and worked with, quiet confidence beats loud confidence any day of the week. The kind of confidence where you don't always feel the need to say something or force your point across. The kind of confidence that recognizes trust is everything and encourages people to speak freely and openly. The kind of confidence where you just listen and let others talk. Ask most seasoned executives and entrepreneurs, and they'll mirror this message by saying quiet people are the most dangerous in the room.

I know this is easier said than done as we all have our own unique challenges to overcome. But people don't care nearly as much about what you do compared to what you can do for them. To enhance your self-worth and boost your confidence, focus on situations where you feel at ease while engaging in conversations that prioritize the comfort of others. Recognize that imperfections play a vital role in showcasing your humanity.

QUESTION YOUR PERCEIVED WEAKNESSES

Stories hold tremendous power. But no story is more powerful than the one we tell ourselves. For the first twenty-three years of my life, I thought I was damaged. I was convinced I'd never amount to anything. The story I told myself of what I was capable of achieving was dominated by an internal narrative of not being enough. The times I was called "stupid," "nerd,"—or the one that sent me into a silent rage, "retard"—only reinforced this narrative. Not to mention that time when a teacher came up to me in front of my new classmates during the first week of school and said, "Hi, M-M-Mike, H-H-o-w-w are y-y-ou?" with a cheeseburger smile on his face. Seeing some of the other teachers and students laughing along convinced me I was destined to be a walking punchline. As these experiences and the stories I told myself stacked, the deeper they became ingrained in how I viewed myself.

Seeing other people own their shyness in the sales job was instrumental in viewing my "perceived" drawbacks through a different lens. It inspired me to question the stories that dominated my internal chatter. Before this self-audit, I viewed myself as the epitome of weak. What I began to slowly realize was that I was looking at myself from the wrong angle. I dared to go back to school the next day after being humiliated and I had the stones to pursue a sales job despite knowing full well it may not be the best fit for someone who stuttered. If anything, these decisions were extremely brave.

The same goes for dissecting the negative connotation of "shyness" as someone who's introverted or reserved. Should we have to justify not being outgoing all the time? Is quietness a weakness? Why equate these connotations as being small or less than? It's absurd when you think about it. Differences give the world color. Depending on the circumstances, even the most confident, outgoing person can be shy. Plus, the key to any success I had in sales was because I *didn't* talk very much.

The shift of viewing myself through the lens of "I'm curious," "I'm brave," and "I care enough to listen," instead of "I'm too shy," "I'm too sensitive," and "I'll never amount to anything," wasn't immediate. The stories we tell ourselves are hard to rewrite. But over time, questioning these self-defeating narratives rather than blindly accepting them, helped me stand more comfortably in my own skin.

But it's not just reexamining the story we tell ourselves that's worth the effort. It's also questioning who we view as valuable in society. We tend to equate the loudest to the strongest or most popular. Some of my closest friends are extroverted. Some are even unbelievably charismatic. But that's not why I like them. I like them because they answer their phones on a Tuesday afternoon when I call, they're interested in what I'm up to, and they pick me up when I fall. They give me the greatest gift you can receive from a friend: the space to be myself.

If you think about the people you most appreciate in your life, I'd bet that like me, it's those who save you from having to reach for a mask to fit in. In her best-selling book *Captivate*, author Vanessa Van Edwards shares a study that backs up the lesson my son's teacher shared with me in the introduction of this book, where the quiet kids were seen as the most valuable to their peers. The study's findings show the most-liked kids in high school weren't the best-looking, most athletic, or so-called cool kids. The underlying quality for the most-liked students is they simply liked their peers and wanted to do good by them.[1]

Whether it's first grade, high school, your neighborhood, the office, or even a sales pit, the most valuable people take the time to understand what other people value. They're supportive. They're interested. They listen.

Looking back, it wasn't my shyness that held me back from making connections with people and pursuing my goals. Nor was it my stutter. The biggest problem was the internal dialogue going on inside my head. I became so wrapped up in what I was going to say, what other people thought about me, and so worried about the million and one ways I'd make a fool of myself, I didn't pay attention to what those around me had to say or what they wanted to achieve.

Through this self-audit and casting aside societal expectations that I previously allowed to dictate my worth, I began to view myself through a new lens and discovered an astonishing revelation in the process—I was already enough. In that moment of profound clarity, instead of attempting to reinvent or mold myself into someone I wasn't, I chose to embrace my true self.

I'm a big believer that the best way to carve our own path is by helping other people carve theirs. But we don't need a cape to accomplish this. Nor do we need to be oozing with confidence and charisma. We need to identify the positive qualities that we possess—of which we have many—while limiting the urge to define ourselves by the qualities we think we lack. Putting ourselves out into the world can be scary. But it doesn't have to be. We can design circumstances that allow us to thrive. Fortunately, there are more of these opportunities than we realize. There's a good chance you're already doing a lot of things right when getting to know other people.

Prioritize Comfort over Confidence

Growing up, I was surrounded by military personnel due to my dad's job. The instructions to make a strong first impression were to pull your shoulders back, take on a wide stance, hold your chin high, and if you're going to shake someone's hand, aim to break it. The more I heard these instructions repeated, the more I believed they were how I should act. There was only one problem: it wasn't me. Not even close. But did I need to buy into this narrative?

Don't get me wrong, there are times when our environment demands a more confident persona. But not every encounter needs to be treated like we're meeting with a venture capitalist or interviewing for a job at a maximum security prison. Most of our day-to-day interactions are looked upon more favorably if we lead with warmth. Consider these two encounters.

The first person walking toward you has read self-help books. Their superhero posture is nothing short of commanding. Once they get close, they stand directly in front of you. Their chin is up. They've followed the "confident-look" direction manual. Immediately, they introduce themselves and start talking.

However, the second person walking toward you is standing up straight with an open posture but isn't erect like an action figure. Instead of getting in front of you, they position themselves slightly to the side, giving you the freedom to move. They're smiling—as they understand no one wants to be approached by a person with a glum look on their face—but they angle their head down and a touch to the side before calmly and slowly saying hello.

Who of these two people would make you feel more comfortable? Who would you be more open to speaking with? Before you think I'm trying to prove a personal point, the data aligns. There are times when speaking quickly can help you come off as more knowledgeable or confident. But this is room-specific. Even though it may work in a debate, this strategy can backfire when meeting someone new.[2] This is because people need time to get a read on both you and what you're saying. The same goes for strong posture. Studies have shown standing confidently can send positive messages to the human brain.[3] But when approaching someone, especially if you're tall or have an imposing presence, consider docking it down a little and aim for inviting rather than intimidating.

If you remember just one thing, stand to the side above all else. Human beings covet the choice to make their own decisions, and blocking or impeding their way sends a negative message. Keep your eyes open to their body language and attempt to match their facial gestures and tone of voice because people like those who share similar mannerisms. The last thing you want to do is approach someone with champagne energy when it's clear they aren't in the mood to celebrate.

If your baseline is going in strong and it works for you, do you. But if your default is less aggressive and you are a bit hesitant when approaching people, rather than beat yourself up over not having a commanding presence, embrace being someone who aims to ensure other people feel comfortable in your presence. Or, better yet, don't go into conversations cold at all. That's the beauty of the world we live in. To feel more confident when speaking with new people, there are plenty of ways to collect easy wins.

Start Where You're Most at Ease

I've lived across three continents and a dozen different towns or cities. In each new place, I have to be proactive in making friends. Through these experiences, I've stumbled upon a practice that allows me to comfortably make connections within my community. Despite not drinking alcohol anymore, I grab a seat at a bar near my house a few times a week for lunch. The rationale? Bartenders and servers are often well-connected in their communities and they are paid to get to know you while creating an environment that encourages you to return. If you make it a regular thing, you can not only continue a previous conversation with the staff, but it also increases the odds of being introduced to other patrons. After all, it's much easier for people to want to talk with you if you're already engaged in a friendly conversation. If you get jumbled or feel like you didn't make a connection, one thing the world doesn't have a shortage of is bars.

We often forget there are professions where conversation is the norm. We can also practice with shop assistants, hairdressers, or any type of customer service or salesperson. Observe them. Get to know them. Each time I buy something, I joke that I just found the debit card on the street and can't believe the PIN worked. Sometimes the joke goes over their heads. The majority of the time, though, it gets a laugh from not only the cashier but the other customers around me. Living now in Spain, making small talk is my secret weapon; on any given day, I'm the lone American in people's orbit which opens the door to talk about the differences between the United States and Spain, which can be a lot of fun.

Consider the times we live in. Heads down and phones out—most of us are oblivious to the world around us, including our fellow human beings. That's why basic human gestures like smiling, holding doors, saying hello to strangers, and having quick interactions are such powerful gestures. Rather than aimlessly scrolling on Instagram when out in public, consider bringing these old-school habits back. Acknowledging others can help you to stand out without having to show off. Plus, once we uncover a few ways to start conversations that work for us, our job is done, as there's no one stopping us from using the same approach with different people.

EMBRACE THE POWER OF QUICK INTERACTIONS

I've lost count of the number of conversation starters I've tried. The ones I thought sounded uncomfortable ended up being *really* uncomfortable. As an experiment, I once tried the suggestion encouraged in many books, "What does your dream day look like?" When the person answered, "Alone," despite telling them they were my hero, they walked away.

Like a lot of people, I initially shuddered at the idea of having a few planned ice-breakers. However, I learned it's hard to have meaningful conversations without establishing common ground or eliciting a spark of curiosity. When designed properly, a few go-to ice-breakers—or ways to keep the conversation going—net positive results. If you find two or three that work and feel natural to you, as you grow more relaxed using them, you can adjust them with each new person you meet.

But one thing a solid ice-breaker doesn't have to be is mind-blowing, which is something I wish I'd internalized sooner. I used to put a lot of unnecessary pressure on myself to "perform" when meeting someone new. I hadn't yet realized the goal of a first impression is to earn a second conversation. That's it. And the goal of getting the conversation going is to allow people time to get a gauge on you by making your introductory remarks easy to catch.

Contrary to popular opinion, feel free to lead with "How are you doing?" It provides people with time to get a read on you. In addition, it allows for easy follow-up questions to get the conversation moving. After exchanging basic pleasantries, my friend Kim Dabbs, author of *You Belong Here*, likes to ask people she meets, "Where do you call home?" It's a small shift in language from the typical question of "Where are you from?" but it allows people to talk about where they're most comfortable. This can create the space to dive deeper into what it is about these places that bring out the best in them. When attending a networking event, asking someone what they would normally be doing after work accomplishes similar results to Kim's question. It opens the door to learn about their hobbies, making it a nice option to ask people in place of "What do you do?"

As someone who prides themselves on their observation skills, I tend to start conversations in one of three ways: making a note of the environment we're in, mentioning an observation like a book someone is reading, or asking a question that has worked well in the past.

The way I use this method as a teacher and writer who loves learning people's life lessons is I'll mention something like, "I'm on my way to pick up my kids, but I'm writing an article [or teaching a class at a university] and I'm asking as many people as I can for a tip regarding [insert nonintrusive topic like the best decision they've made in their career]." You don't need to be a writer, either. It's just as effective to remark, "My friends and I have been talking about [insert an easy-to-grasp topic] and I'd love to learn your thoughts." This simple lead-in kills a lot of birds with one stone.

First, most people have an opinion on career advice, and the topic isn't polarizing or too personal. If they struggle to answer, share a few pieces of advice you've heard from other people or mention your own. When starting a conversation, you can even comment on the weather as a conversation starter. Everyone has an opinion on it, and I've never once thought to myself after a quality conversation—"She was cool, but that comment about it being cloudy was pure lunacy!" When meeting new people, their heads are already running in circles trying to guess your intentions. Find a few simple lead-ins to give people time to catch up to the circumstances. It's hard to reach the deep conversations we yearn for without first wading through the shallow end of the pool.

Second, even though a lot of experts suggest keeping the focus 100 percent on the other person, which is mostly correct, depending on the situation and personality type, it can be helpful to drop a little bit of information about yourself early on in the conversation. The logic: What if they're also shy? Or perhaps they aren't comfortable telling a stranger about themselves? Call me crazy, but I want to know about the people who approach me as quickly as possible. That's why I'll remark that I have kids, and I'm a writer interested in career advice.

Third, the bit—"I'm on my way to pick up my kids"—lowers defenses. As a survival mechanism, we're hardwired to determine if people around us are a threat. According to Robin Dreeke, the former head of the FBI's Behavioral Analysis Program and author of *It's Not All About "Me,"* there's a very simple way to make people feel comfortable: let them know you won't take up much of their time. In Robin's words, "The first step in the process of developing great rapport and having great conversations is letting the other person know that there is an end in sight, and it is really close."[4]

Robin's wisdom has been a godsend for not only me but also countless students and clients. For example, "I have to meet my wife in five minutes, but I've heard good things about the book you're reading." "I have to get to a meeting. But I'm curious. . . . " Not only do these simple phrases help people relax, they bring positive energy to the interaction because they know the conversation won't drag on. Even better, it provides you with an easy out if things go south. At the same time, it can be a chance to make plans to connect later if things are going well—"I have to get back to work, but I really enjoyed getting to know you and I hope we can meet again."

REMEMBER, THOUGHTFULNESS IS FOREVER COOL

Two decades have passed since I took the leap and pursued a sales job to stand more comfortably in my own skin and build connections with people. This one decision led me on a path I never imagined I'd have the confidence to walk down. I'm proud of what I've been able to accomplish. I never would have thought I'd be sought out by people to hone their communication skills and better bet on themselves.

However, I'm convinced with every ounce of my being my life would have taken a radically different turn if my manager hadn't offered me the space to find my own way. It's funny the moments that hit us and the seemingly "small" actions of others that stick with us. When I heard the corporate trainer shout "Role plays," during my first week on the job, I was moments away from calling it quits. By pulling me aside and suggesting I find my comfort zone on my own terms, my manager played a pivotal role in allowing me to uncover my strengths without having to display my perceived weaknesses for the world to see. His encouragement to get curious regarding how I was best positioned to lead myself ultimately influenced how I would eventually choose to lead others.

I've traveled the globe since leaving that job. I've met and worked with thousands of individuals and hundreds of organizations as an entrepreneur, teacher, and consultant. Sure, some of the more confident and charismatic people I've met stand out in my memory. But even more pronounced in my mind's eye are the thoughtful ones.

Those like my first boss who led with warmth and consideration.

Those who were there for me when I needed them and lifted me up when I fell.

Most of all, those who possessed a rare gift—their unwavering commitment to listen.

Lead with Listening

"WE'RE GOING TO DO SOMETHING DIFFERENT TODAY. RATHER than talking, we're going to watch videos and I want you to write down three things you learn from each person in the conversations."

A speech therapist said this to me at the beginning of one of our sessions. I thought she'd lost her mind. I was there for her to help me talk, and here she was asking me to watch TV and take notes. Despite my confusion, I was half-tempted to shut up and do what I was told as it sounded like a nice reprieve from our normal sessions of me turning into a bright red tomato trying to recite tongue twisters. But my curiosity got the best of me. And I'm glad it did because her rationale for the exercise changed my life.

"Your problem isn't speaking," she began. "Your challenge, like a lot of people, is you get so caught up in what you're going to say and how other people perceive you, you don't truly listen to anyone. To connect with others, you have to quiet your internal chatter and put your agenda aside."

Upon hearing these words, I had to stop myself from arguing back. I prided myself on my listening skills. I used to tell people since I couldn't talk very well that I was a good listener. And now I was being told that I was bad at the one thing I thought I was good at. But the more I thought about her words, the more my eyes opened to the truth of what she was saying. Due to the constant pressure I put myself under to "perform," and not embarrass myself, I went into most conversations thinking solely about me.

Once this session was over, I thought it'd be the last of the note-taking exercises. But it was just the beginning. Each time we met, we'd spend fifteen minutes watching videos before discussing the observations I'd written down regarding both the verbal and nonverbal communication displayed. As daily homework, she encouraged me to continue the habit of jotting down three things I learned about someone after each real-world conversation I had.

It's funny how sometimes the annoying or frustrating things we're recommended to do end up being the exact advice we need. Being told you need to be a better listener is a lot like being told you should eat more broccoli. However, the benefits of prioritizing this skill are undeniable. Throughout my career, no matter where I was in the world or which sector I was working in, one pattern remained consistent: the truly valuable people around me were those who took the time to identify what was most valuable to the people around them.

I still carry my notebook with me everywhere I go to write down a few details about each person I speak with, like their kids' names, their passion projects, a challenge they're facing, or something they have coming up in their lives that's important to them. This habit kills quite a few birds with one stone.

- First, always carrying a notebook serves as a spark to get curious.

- Second, it ensures you won't forget what you observe and learn.

- Third, the phrase, "I love that thought, do you mind if I write it down so I don't forget it?" goes over well.

- Last, keeping a to-do list of what other people are up to opens the door for quick check-ins to see how things are going.

But listening isn't just about hearing or remembering. It's also about connecting and understanding. In other words, listening is a mix of curiosity and empathy—which are the keys to being able to truly see others.

I internalized this lesson the first time I spoke with my friend and career coach Rafa Sarandeses when he said, "Our time isn't the greatest gift we can give to someone; our presence is." He went on to add that it allows us to absorb and better understand what people are saying, which opens the door to asking relevant follow-up questions that dig deeper into their experiences.

I thought Rafa's wisdom was really smart. While everyone is vying for attention, the way he carefully crafted his words reminded me of the oldest trick in the book when it comes to building relationships: choosing to be the type of person who's attentive to others.

If you think about the best conversations of your life, the moments someone left a great first impression on you, or simply thought you'd like to spend more time with someone upon hanging out with them, I'd bet the undercurrent to these interactions is they cared enough to listen and they were present. We may not think to ourselves, "That conversation was amazing, they were super present!" but we feel it—and what gets felt gets remembered.

Like anything that sounds nice, suspending our ego and putting our agenda aside in favor of prioritizing the person in front of us is hard. That's why it's valuable. We often feel the need to compete, compare, and sometimes demonstrate a position of power by one-upping, interrupting, or flat-out boosterism. When this isn't happening, many of us worry about what we're going to say, how people are labeling us, and whether or not they like us. The fact we now have in our pockets arguably the most addictive device ever created—our smartphones—doesn't help. But all these internal mind games and digital distractions do is impede us from listening to people.

Building connections with people is an art, and like with all art, everyone will have a different interpretation. For me, its essence lies in creating the space for people to reveal themselves. It's setting the foundation for identifying how your story and the story of the person in front of you best collide. And in this, listening plays the starring role.

DESIGNING CONVERSATION PERSONAS

Much of the advice we're given to be a *better* listener is to be an *active* listener. I agree that listening is a verb. But it's also a conscious choice. It's a mindset we carry with us. Very few people go into interactions to be the best listener in the room, making it a surefire way to quietly stand out. It's impossible to think we'll always get it right as the world we live in is one giant distraction and it's not always easy to get out of our own heads. But if there was one skill worth pursuing and making our forever work, this would be it.

My technique to make active listening truly active in conversations is to adopt specific personas that serve as a reminder to put my own agenda aside and dig into the people's dreams, fears, hopes, and desires. Here are five personas that I've used that can help you better focus on the person in front of you. Not only have they allowed me to move from someone terrified of meeting people to making a living by helping them to better express themselves, but they make listening fun. Great things happen when we ask ourselves, "What could I learn if I just kept listening?"

BE A FEATHER

One of the best pieces of communication advice I've ever received came at the hands of a woman I barely understood—my first Spanish teacher. She demanded that my classmates and I sit in silence for three minutes at the beginning of each class. Though quirky, her logic was genius. It's impossible to learn a language if you're preoccupied and not fully immersed in the present moment.

I'm sure being alive two hundred years ago wasn't easy, but our modern world often feels out of control. Among work, money, family, health issues, trying to maintain some semblance of a social life, and trying to keep up with how quickly the world is changing—it's amazing we have the headspace to listen to anyone.

It's not just our present concerns and future worries that pull us away from being in the moment in conversations. We may not think about it very much, but we all carry with us a vast catalog of past experiences that silently influence our present interactions. I worry about what I'm going to say and how I'm going to say it. As a survival mechanism, I pretended that the jabs I received growing up and early on in my career didn't hurt. But they did hurt. They destroyed my confidence and made me feel stupid. Whether I realized it or not, at times these experiences made me skeptical of others and held me back from truly letting people into my life.

The more we can unpack these concerns, however, and enter a conversation in a state of lightness—like a feather—the better we can create the space for connections with others. As my Spanish teacher alluded to, if our cup is already full of our worries, it becomes hard to make room to learn about and from others.

Maybe you carry concerns about money with you. Or maybe the mental boulder that impedes you from listening is work stress. Or maybe at times, like me, you worry too much about what other people think of you and perhaps you have trouble shaking the times you felt like a fool. Take inventory for one week of the thoughts and worries you consistently carry into conversations that pull you away from truly listening to people. Write them down. Track your internal chatter to see if you can spot some baggage that consistently shows up when approaching conversations.

This isn't about downplaying the importance of these thoughts, worries, and concerns. They're valid. It's about choosing to put them aside in the moment so you can better zero in on the person in front of you. By choosing the mindset of a feather, the door opens for us to be blown away by the people we meet.

BE A SET DESIGNER

When I began teaching leadership and communication to students pursuing their master's, I was encouraged to "dress the part" of a lecturer by wearing a suit. Fortunately, after explaining my goal was to find equal footing with the students as quickly as possible so they felt like they could speak freely, I didn't have to go out and buy a tie.

The school I teach at has the typical old-school classroom setup with white walls, glossy windows, fluorescent lighting, and rows of desks which make group work a chore. It's a stark contrast to another school I worked at where the seats were placed in a circle and the room was filled with lots of natural light and inspiring art on the walls. It was shocking to observe how much these environments affected the behavior of the students. One was primed for a "lecture," and the other was geared toward creativity and collaboration. Being a firm believer that maximizing creativity and collaboration is key to new world leadership, it didn't come as a surprise that the uncomfortable room demanded more work from both me and the students.

I wish I had learned about designing comfortable environments earlier in my career. Sure, it's not always possible to drastically overhaul our physical environment. But taking the time to think about the aspects you can control serves as a trigger to prioritize the comfort of others. Think about it: If you have to give a performance review or give someone bad news, which environment do you think creates a more comfortable atmosphere for a potentially uncomfortable conversation? Sitting behind your office desk in a high-back chair while the person sits in front of you in a lower-positioned chair? Or sitting next to them in the same style of chairs at a round table so you're on equal ground?

Although a small shift, the difference between "Take a seat" that's typically said in the office desk scenario compared to "Join me" provides psychological safety for people. The same goes for brainstorming outside or taking a walk compared to sitting in a stuffy room. Ideas tend to grow legs when we're physically moving.

Think about how people like to be treated and the circumstances that led to great conversations in the past. "Where" matters. Environment affects our behavior much more than we often realize. There's a reason many therapists have warm spaces and creative teams opt to not have their offices in business parks where all the buildings look the same.

BE A BIOGRAPHER

The goal of every great conversationalist I know is to learn the stories of others. One common recommendation to accomplish this is by asking "So, what's your story?" This may make logical sense. And it works for some of my friends. But I don't know about you (and don't get me wrong, but much like "Tell me about yourself" in interviews, it's important to know how to navigate the question), I've always felt uncomfortable being asked this question immediately upon meeting someone. This is especially true if it's in a group setting, as it's a spotlight question, and bright lights aren't for me. Plus, I've asked not only friends, but also hundreds of students and thousands of my readers if they feel comfortable when people ask it, and more times than not, I'm met with a moan. It's too much too soon. Depending on the circumstances, we struggle with where to begin. So rather than putting the spotlight on someone immediately, remind yourself to gently guide them to it.

We're going to be digging into this in further detail in the next chapter—"Treat Your Curiosity as Your Primary Responsibility"—but for starters, pretend your job when meeting with someone is to *slowly* piece together their biography. After exchanging basic pleasantries, consider asking questions that are easy for people to catch and allow you to learn about their experiences, interests, and tastes to see if you share any overlap.

Feel free to start with general topics like food or travel to get conversations moving. Asking a question about what kind of music people were into during high school allows them to think back to what they were like growing up while opening the door to learning how their tastes have evolved. The same goes for inquiring about what someone studied in school compared to what they are doing today. To get conversations going or to pick up the energy if they begin to fizzle, May Pang, a friend who writes beautiful articles on navigating growing up shy and now works as a connection coach, often asks people for their first childhood memory that comes to mind. She doesn't stipulate whether the memory should be good or bad while giving people the space to ponder the question. The options are endless, ranging from asking people what topic they would discuss if they had the chance to give a talk that all the world would see to asking them if they have any hobbies they regret quitting. These questions get people talking about topics they are interested in or what they were like as a kid. Doing so opens the door to asking specific follow-up questions to dive deeper into their background and experiences.

My friend and talented storyteller, Todd Brison, said it well: "As an introvert, it helps me to think of each person not as a person, but as a living story, decades in the making. My only job is to extract the story." But remember, you don't need to get it all in one hit. Biographers take years to research someone and collect bits of their story one piece at a time. Taking note of these experiences and saying, "The last time we talked you mentioned . . . " demonstrates you're not only listening but that you care and you're curious to learn more about their experiences. Bringing the mindset of "I'm going to learn something I didn't previously know about this person" into each conversation can revolutionize your relationships.

Be a Trampoline

Like a lot of people, I fell into the advice of being like a sponge to soak up as much as I could about the person I was speaking with when I began to understand the tremendous value of listening. Don't get me wrong; there are worse aspirations. Leadership experts Jack Zenger and Joseph Folkman, however, say it's not enough. In their insightful article in *Harvard Business Review*, titled "What Great Listeners Actually Do," which gleaned insights from 3,492 participants to pin down the distinguishing factors that separate average and good listeners from great ones, they shared the following.

> While many of us have thought of being a good listener being like a sponge that accurately absorbs what the other person is saying, instead, what these findings show is that good listeners are like trampolines. They are someone you can bounce ideas off of—and rather than absorbing your ideas and energy, they amplify, energize, and clarify your thinking. They make you feel better not merely passively absorbing, but by actively supporting. This lets you gain energy and height, just like someone jumping on a trampoline.[1]

I don't know about you, but I love that visual. The imagery of raising both the person you are speaking with and the conversation to a higher level is powerful. We're going to be diving into the type of questions to make this happen in the following chapter, but for starters, remind yourself that conversations are a two-way street. Rather than creating an empty space for people to bounce their own ideas around, bounce ideas back by asking thoughtful questions and sharing your own experiences on the topic.

Be a Smart Parrot

When my friend Nick Wignal, perhaps the best listener I've ever met, began studying to be a psychologist, he shuddered at the idea of being a "reflective" listener. However, it didn't take him long to see the value of it. Reflective listening isn't simply repeating what people say, but taking a moment before summarizing what you've heard in your own words. Hence, a smart parrot that can put one plus one together.

For example, if someone is going on about how awful their boss is and how much work they have on their plate, rather than downplay their feelings, one-up them with your own challenges, or offer advice on how to fix it, and summarize what you heard. This could come in the form of "It sounds like you're overwhelmed from . . . " or, "It seems like you have a lot on your plate. . . . "

This may feel or sound condescending. But it's not about the information, it's about people feeling understood and connected. As human beings, we love solving problems. When someone is sharing with you their worries and concerns, we want to jump in and help. Although well-intentioned, this can often backfire, and much of the time when people talk, they simply need to let things out. For Nick, there's a massive clue whether people want to talk or whether they want advice—*they ask for it.*

Adopt the mindset of a smart parrot. When people are talking, let them know you're listening by occasionally summarizing what they've said. The phrase, "What I'm hearing . . . " also allows people to dial in to ensure they're communicating correctly, and if not, it gives them space to clarify themselves. If you don't understand something, Denise Young Smith, former Chief of Human Resources at Apple, recommends saying, "This is new to me and I want to understand it. Can we start again?" which I think is a nice way of letting people know you care.

It hadn't dawned on me until speaking with Nick that reflective listening is a big part of my job as a teacher and coach. On any given day, I'm helping people work through how they feel about something and simplifying their often complicated thoughts. For any sort of progress to be made in these interactions, my students and clients have to feel like they are being seen and heard. Summarizing back what I am hearing demonstrates that I'm actively looking to better understand them while giving them the space to speak freely and better express themselves.

If people want anything, it's to feel validated. For Nick, when this happens, all sorts of good things start to happen, no matter how bad the situation is.

ABOVE ALL, BE THE OPPOSITE OF A CRICKET

All great listeners take the time to think before they speak while also recognizing when they don't need to speak at all. When getting to know and discussing what impedes people from listening, Warren Schaefer, a three-time startup founder, said something I agree with the first time we spoke, "Society as a whole has a problem with silence." He went on to add that we get uncomfortable and feel like we immediately need to chime in.

The urge to give unsolicited advice, finish someone's thought, or reach for our phone to not have to face the discomfort that silence can often create is real. But we need time to digest what we're hearing and better understand where someone is coming from and they need time to formulate their thoughts and feelings. Just because someone isn't immediately replying to a question you asked doesn't mean they don't have an answer. It could be they're giving you the gift of how they can best express themselves. Life isn't a game of *Jeopardy* where we have to immediately jump in with a response—or even respond at all. Silence creates space and space is good.

Think about how you can create an environment for people to reveal more of themselves to you. Observe them. Remind yourself that presence builds connections and our words are most impactful when we take the time to understand what other people value.

The more attentive we are to the people around us and the more curious we are about their stories, the better we can identify how our worlds can best collide.

PRINCIPLE 3

Treat Your Curiosity as Your Primary Responsibility

A SCENE IN THE HIT SERIES *TED LASSO* MADE ME PAUSE AND grab my notebook. The premise of the show is Ted leaves his job as the head coach of a college football team in the United States to become head coach for a soccer team in the United Kingdom, despite not knowing anything about the sport. When envisioning Lasso's character, imagine a guy who looks like Ned Flanders from the *Simpsons* and speaks like a comedic version of TED Talks darling and author of the hit book *Start with Why*, Simon Sinek. Empathetic. Witty. Superb storyteller. Magnificent mustache.

The villain in the scene that caught my eye is the soccer club's millionaire former owner, who lost the team to his ex-wife because of their divorce settlement. Not being able to leave his club alone, he gives his new girlfriend a bucket of money to buy ownership in the club so he'll continue to have a say in the board of directors' decisions.

Despite Ted slowly winning over some players and fans, the antagonist still sees him as a walking punchline and thinks he's running the club into the ground. The two men agree to settle an argument through a game of darts in the local pub. If Ted's nemesis wins, he can pick the starting lineup for the remaining two matches of the year, and if Ted wins, the villain has to disappear and stop being a thorn in his ex-wife's side.

The match is tight. Going into the last round, the villain has an edge. Ted needs to hit two twenties and a double bull's-eye to win with his last three throws, which is no easy task. The bar is buzzing. The millionaire is convinced he's already won. But then, just as Ted prepares to throw the first dart, in typical Lasso fashion, he shares a story.

"Guys have underestimated me my entire life," he begins while eyeing the dartboard. "And for years I never understood why—it used to really bother me. Then, one day, I was driving my little boy to school, and I saw a quote by Walt Whitman. It was painted on the wall and it said, 'Be curious, not judgmental.' I like that."

Ted throws a dart and hits one of the two twenties. The crowd goes berserk.

"So, I get back in my car," Ted continues, "and I'm driving to work and all of a sudden it hits me—all them fellas that used to belittle me, not a single one of them was curious. You know, they thought they had everything all figured out, so they judged everything, and they judged everyone. And I realized that their underestimating me—who I was had nothing to do with it. Because if they were curious, they would've asked questions. Questions like, 'Have you played a lot of darts, Ted?'"

Ted coolly throws another dart and lands the second of the two twenties he needs.

"To which I would have answered, 'Yes sir. Every Sunday afternoon at a sports bar with my father from age ten until I was sixteen when he passed away.'"

Ted then zeros in and, to the astonishment of the crowd, crushes a double bull's-eye to win the bet while muttering his trademark phrase under his breath, "Barbeque sauce."[1]

BE CURIOUS, NOT JUDGMENTAL

Ted's got a lot going for him. He's charming. He understands the importance of remembering people's names. He knows how to spin a story. It's not a surprise the TV show dominated headlines when it first came out as Ted is the friend and boss most people would love to have by their side.

Even though he doesn't initially know anything about soccer, his ego is nonexistent, and he learns the technical aspects of the sport from the kit man, no less, as he lays down lesson after lesson about the human side of leadership. But perhaps his greatest quality is he sees the absolute best in everyone and works to bring out their strengths while minimizing their weaknesses. In short, he leaves each person feeling bigger about themselves than he found them. Unlike his judgmental opponent, who couldn't imagine that an American football coach could possibly beat him at English darts, Lasso accomplishes this because—whether he's speaking with his boss, the groundskeepers, or even the press—he leads with curiosity.

I bet you've experienced your own Ted Lasso moments like in the dart scene where you didn't feel seen, heard, or valued. I'm sure there have also been times when people either judged you, underestimated you, or flat-out disrespected you. Perhaps it was because of your race, age, nationality, appearance, accent, style, tattoos, or you have a name some people aren't willing to learn how to pronounce. Maybe it was because a time you put yourself out into the world your work, values, or beliefs were met with critique as criticizing others is the easy choice.

I'm not going to pretend like I don't judge people. I do, and so do you. It's part of the human condition. We may say things like "Don't judge a book by its cover" to our kids to remind them of the importance of being open-minded and not labeling someone without taking their entirety into consideration. But this cliché doesn't represent how humans operate. We actively judge others. Since the days of wolves, lions, and marauding tribes, the ones who weren't judgmental didn't last very long. An argument can be made that we're the offspring of the most judgmental people the world has known—because that's how our ancestors survived long enough to have families.

For many of us today, however, our biggest concerns aren't so much about survival as they are about finding ways to thrive. Sometimes, we need to listen to the messages our body and brain are sending us. But there are also several times during our run-of-the-mill interactions where the work isn't to do away with judgment but to suspend it to give people the space to get a fair shake. Or, as writer Barry Davret shared in an insightful featured *Medium* article, to judge "thoughtfully."[2]

In any situation, the only thing that is certain is that very little is certain. We see a snapshot, never the full picture. The woman approaching us with a warm smile may very well be a serial killer, whereas the bearded man with tattoos wearing sunglasses at night in a park may be blind. We don't have enough initial information to draw accurate conclusions. This doesn't mean we should immediately give someone who feels like a threat a free pass; we have gut checks for a reason that are worth listening to. However, it's important to step back and remind ourselves that every one of us has more to offer than meets the eye at the first, second, or even third glance. There is more depth than just initial appearances, and at our core, we all share the same desire to feel seen and heard and be valued.

When people discover I'm a communication consultant and teach leadership, they expect one thing: a strong, confident, and powerful persona. What they get is quite the opposite. I stutter, which many people view as a weakness. I'm also authentically uncertain and gravitate toward corners during networking events. Some people may even think I have bladder problems because I spent a lot of time in the bathroom at parties to get a breather and play the word game Spelling Bee on my phone.

Fortunately, there are enough people in the world who are curious why someone who—on paper—shouldn't be in the communication world, is. I can't tell you how impactful that's been. And our goal should be to do the same for others.

A TALE OF TWO EMAILS

Shortly after I began writing, I received two emails from two different people who said two very different things. The first message went on a tirade about how idiotic an article I'd recently published was. This person told me I was embarrassing myself by sharing my thoughts and stories online. Even though I've been around long enough to know I'm not for everyone, the comment stung. The worst part? I knew the person who emailed. We used to hang out when I lived in the United States, and I didn't know he'd been reading my articles or forming an opinion about my writing.

The article he referenced involved suggestions for phrases not to say to people in conversations. In his message, he mentioned "the irony" of being someone who stutters while teaching others how to talk. Despite the article consisting of not only my suggestions but recommendations from communication experts from an array of diverse backgrounds, his comment was hard to shake.

A few days later, however, I received a different message that surprised me. The email came from Denise Young Smith, the former Chief of Human Resources at Apple, asking to get to know me. Her reason? She loved the same article that the other man ridiculed me about. She said it reminded her of a module she taught while serving as the Entrepreneur-in-Residence at Cornell Tech titled "Words Matter."

I'll never forget her email. Here was someone more successful, with the means to speak to just about anyone in the world, but she chose to spend her time getting to know some random person in Spain who wrote an article she liked on the internet.

Before our call, I researched Denise as well as I could. The fact *Business Insider* had named her as one of the one hundred most influential people in Silicon Valley didn't help to calm my nerves. But when Denise and I finished talking, I realized I'd only asked her one of the dozen questions I'd written—because rather than talk about herself, from the time we got on the call till it ended, she dug into me.

Pure curiosity for the person in front of her.

Zero judgment.

No ego whatsoever.

As soon as I answered a question, she'd dig a layer deeper to get to the heart of my drivers, values, and story. "I'm curious. What motivated you to get into this work?" "I'm interested. How did working in that environment make you feel?"

This immediately explained to me how Denise could achieve such great heights in her career, and, as a Black woman in a predominantly white, male-dominated sector, why she'd become "a first and an only." She told me she admired me for having the courage to put myself out into the world, that the world needed more empathetic voices like mine, and that her door was always open. Despite being six thousand miles away, she made me feel as if she was sitting right beside me.

Being on the receiving end of Denise's curiosity—and getting a reminder of how good that felt compared to the man's message that aimed to make me feel small—I received a memorable lesson on the importance of being curious and asking people questions that get to the heart of who they are.

EMBRACE EXPLORER QUESTIONS TO CREATE CONNECTIONS

It's not a secret that to make connections with people you'll have to ask them questions. But all questions aren't created equal. When growing curious about someone, the type of questions I recommend are "exploration" questions. Similar to open-ended questions, exploration questions encourage people to expand on aspects of a conversation so we can gain a deeper understanding of their thoughts, beliefs, ideas, feelings, and experiences. In contrast, closed questions only allow for a limited range of responses, such as "yes," "no," or "I don't know." The key difference between "exploration" and "open-ended" questions is slight but important. It's a helluva lot more fun to remind yourself to be an explorer of others than it is to remind yourself to be the type of person who asks open-ended questions.

For example, if someone is talking about their career, a closed question would look something like, "Do you like your job?" whereas an exploratory question would be something like, "I'm curious, how did you end up in this line of work?" Exploratory questions say, "I'm interested. Tell me more!" But perhaps the biggest reason they are more effective than asking closed questions is even if it's not your intention, closed questions can often make people feel defensive or like they're being judged. Imagine you walk into your house after a long day and you immediately ask your partner, "Is dinner ready?" or the question that drives my wife bonkers, "Have the kids had their baths yet?" Maybe you had zero intention of making them feel defensive, but the odds are high that if they say no, they'll either feel the need to justify why dinner isn't on the table or remind you a divorce attorney is a search away.

Similar to the style in which Denise Young Smith guided our conversation, here are a few examples of solid exploratory questions that allow people to reveal themselves:

- "I'm curious. What was it like to . . . ?"
- "This is new to me. Can you help me understand . . . ?"
- "That took a lot of guts. What motivated you to . . . ?"
- "That couldn't have been easy. I'm curious. What steps did you take to . . . ?"

- "I hadn't considered that. What is it about that option that . . . ?
- "That's interesting. Can you tell me a little more about that?"

These types of questions keep the focus on the other person without making them feel like they're being interrogated, which opens the door for them to open up with you. There are two critical notes to keep in mind when asking exploratory questions. First, you may have noticed that before each question is a padding statement, or what some people refer to as "transition" statements (i.e., "I'm curious . . . ," "I never thought of it that way," "That's interesting"). According to Barry Davret, the writer I referenced previously regarding "thoughtful judgment" who also carved out a lane for himself in sales despite falling on the shy side, these statements are crucial. Without the prompts, the questions can come off as harsh or abrupt. These transitionary statements help make the conversation more fluid.[3] Second, ensure you're using this technique if you're *actually* interested, which should be easy assuming you're curious about the person. But either way, the difference in tone between saying, "I'm curious . . ." when speaking in a monotone compared to a genuinely interested tone is enormous. You don't want it to sound forced, or worse, condescending.

The primary driver for these questions is to get people to reveal themselves slowly so you learn their story. Once you know someone's experience and why they do what they do, or why they believe what they believe, even if you don't agree with everything they do or say, you'll see their humanity.

THE STRENGTH OF VULNERABILITY

Going back once more to the TV series *Ted Lasso*, throughout the first season, Ted has the impossible task of healing a broken team. It's a team full of players from all over the world with different backgrounds, values, and motivators, not to mention egos. But there's a moment in the show when a shift takes place. To encourage a sense of camaraderie among team members and highlight their shared values despite their differences, Ted suggests each player bring a meaningful item to share with the team and explain why it matters to them.

The first person to go is the middle-aged captain of the team, Roy Kent, who despite having a reputation as being a hardass, is facing the painful reality that his career is coming to a close. The item Roy shares is a blanket. His grandfather gave it to him when he was recruited at age nine to play for a team in the cold north of England. Roy shares that he was not only freezing in this new environment but scared and the blanket meant so much to him because it was the last time he saw his granddad.

A few other players step up and share things like pictures of their home country and the people who mean a great deal to them. To wrap things up, the star of the team, Jamie Tartt, who has a massive ego and constantly butts heads with the captain, Roy Kent, offers a pair of old soccer cleats. He shared in an uncharacteristically soft tone how his mom gave them to him when he was "just a sexy little baby." He said she didn't even care if he was good, she just wanted him to be happy and his motivation was to make her proud. Tartt then went on to add that as he began to improve, his dad would brag to his friends whenever he scored a goal while calling him "soft" if he "didn't dominate." He shared how much he hated that. As a result, he made a vow to be so tough his dad could never call him soft again. He then ended his heartfelt speech by saying in a searching voice, "I wonder sometimes if I forget about making my mom proud. I don't think she would be lately."

Upon sharing these stories, you can feel the shift in the room as the players view each other through a more empathetic lens. But not the type of empathy that often gets construed as sympathy or pity for someone's circumstances—the type of empathy that's rooted in respect and understanding. The type of empathy that understands people don't want to be fixed. They want to be seen and heard and have their existences validated.

The shift within the team didn't lead to immediate world domination. But thanks to the players showing vulnerability, it served as the much-needed catalyst to begin moving forward as a collective. Rather than continue to constantly butt heads, they begin to make concessions *with* each other and *for* each other. They're more patient. Sure, at times captain Roy Kent and superstar Jamie Tartt get on each other's nerves. But the stories they shared set the foundation for growing in curiosity for the lived experience of each other, which ultimately, leads to authentically wanting to support each other.

Stories are the great human connector. They're the world's strongest bridge. When we take the time to discover other people's stories, we see parts in others that aren't only similar to us, but exactly *like* us. We discover that we're all human beings filled with fears, aspirations, goals, values, and emotions that define the human experience and our shared yearning to do some good in the world. Our backgrounds, dreams, and titles may vary, but we all have the same job: *to create the space for stories to take place.* And this all starts with curiosity—not judgment—for the lived experience of others. Like Roy Kent and Jamie Tartt demonstrate as their relationship shifts from enemies to allies, it's hard to root against someone when you know their story.

You Judge, You Lose

The master's program where I teach is located ninety minutes away from my home. Each time I go, I have to prepare and deliver a five-hour session and between travel, meals, and parking, the gig may end up costing me more money than I make. *The reason I do it?* The students teach me just as much—if not more—than I teach them. If they don't, then I know I'm not doing my job.

My last class had forty-three students hailing from thirty-seven different countries. Iceland. Nigeria. Italy. Bulgaria. Canada. Iran.

Colombia. Egypt. Romania. Their backgrounds vary and the systems they're coming from range from slightly bent to flat-out broken.

To set the stage and create the environment for stories to take place in the class, before the course I send a welcome message with a few details of my story and the challenges I've faced. I then recommend they connect with me on LinkedIn so I can get an overview of their background and they can learn a bit more about me. Last, as an early homework assignment, not to be discussed for a few classes (or at all, if they're not comfortable), I ask them to think about the following three questions:

- What is one of the defining moments of your life (good or bad)?
- What is your "why" or motivator for doing what you do?
- What is one person or piece of advice that has helped you on your way?

I conclude the message by saying the purpose of the course isn't for me to tell them what to do but for us to work together to bring out our strengths and break through some tightly held barriers we are facing.

On the first day of class, I begin by sharing a more detailed version of my story including "My name is M-M-Michael, and I used to sell m-m-m-ortgages," along with a few more bumps and bruises I've incurred along the way. I do this because sharing my story helps them to see me as a person who has also faced challenges. To round things out, I tell them that no matter how many times I've taught, every time I'm terrified of speaking to an audience. To ensure they don't think I'm blowing smoke, I show them my trembling hands and sweat-drenched palms.

This may seem like an odd way to position myself as someone who can help them. But by doing so, something magical happens: they slowly share their own experiences. When they do, the curiosity in the room goes through the roof while any preconceived notions or judgments they are holding onto go out the window.

Think about it. How would you feel about a shy twenty-five-year-old guy from Beirut if you learned he quit his stable job in a very unstable environment to volunteer his skills to rebuild the city after explosions ripped it apart?

What about a young Russian woman who made the terrifying decision to leave her home after the war in Ukraine began and had to rely on the generosity of strangers in neighboring countries to survive, before fighting to find a school that would accept her to live somewhere—*anywhere*—legally?

What about an Indian man who, at age forty-five, came to Spain without his family to study, hoping to find a job that will allow his children to grow up in a first-world country?

What about a young woman from Albania who recently lost her father and quit her job to move to Barcelona to find her superpowers again?

How about a twenty-three-year-old Syrian man who also left his job to volunteer in the war? When asked why he did it, he states, "We volunteer. It's what we do. Community is everything."

What would you think about these people after hearing their stories?

Would you look at them through a new lens?

If you're anything like me, the words "brave" "bold," and most of all, "hero" come to mind. These are actual stories from people you walk by every day. People not like you or me, but also people *just* like you and me. People who have had to overcome challenges and setbacks and are, at times, scared as hell. Yet, they've made something of themselves and are fighting for a life they can be proud of.

If you were to ask most of them for their story, they'd say they don't have one. Like many of us, most of my students have spent a lifetime feeling invisible. By asking them about their experiences with a question as simple as what brought them to Barcelona, it becomes abundantly clear they not only have a story, but one that transcends borders as each of their stories speaks directly to the human experience.

My title may be "Leadership and Communication Lecturer." But my *actual* role is nothing more than to give a damn. It's creating space where they can express who they are, where they came from, and what they are fighting for. The aim is to provide a safe environment for all class members to recognize their inherent worth and draw strength from one another, as they are already strong just the way they are.

These stories of my students may sound like extreme examples. And don't get me wrong, some are. But every one of us has a story, and that means that each person around the globe has one too. Maybe the story of the person who comes from a wealthy family is fighting to find the courage to strike out on their own and step out of their parents' shadow. There's respect for that. Or maybe their driver is to work in the health sector because they lost a loved one to cancer. Perhaps, similar to me, it's not being heard growing up and their fight is to ensure the people around them don't feel that way.

We're going to be diving into how to share your story memorably in Principle 10, "Own Your Story." But for starters, remind yourself that the best way to begin to write your own story is by learning the stories of others. Set the stage for maximum comfort. Explore the origin story of the people you meet. Dig into their values, motivations, or even something that greatly frustrates them about the world. These areas often hold untold stories that are waiting to be unearthed in a thoughtful and considerate manner.

Bringing out the stories of others holds tremendous power, but it doesn't come from being charismatic or confident. Instead, it comes from adopting the principle of treating your curiosity as your primary responsibility. It comes from choosing to give a damn. It comes from listening and asking questions. Questions that set the stage to build authentic connections with people. Questions like—"Do you play a lot of darts, Ted?"

PRINCIPLE 4

Grow Your Confidence in Private

STARING AT THE CLOCK, I DID THE MATH. IF MY CLASSMATE would just keep speaking beyond his ten-minute time limit, I wouldn't have to give my presentation in front of my eleventh-grade history class. He was already at the eight-minute mark. "Come on, man," I pleaded in my head, my left leg twitching. "Don't stop talking! Tell us more about the fascinating life of Margaret Thatcher!"

I watched the clock make another round.

Nine minutes. "Keep going."
Ten minutes. "Come on."
Eleven minutes. "That's it."
Twelve minutes. "This is the greatest day of my life!"

In an instant, the stress and anxiety I'd been storing up since learning we'd have to give a presentation washed off of me. But just as quickly as the euphoria set in, my elation got slammed to the ground. "Thompson," I heard my teacher, Mr. C shout, "You're up. Let's squeeze this in."

When called upon in class, let alone asked to present, I often felt on the verge of passing out. I turned fire-engine red, a stark contrast to my blond hair, resembling a strawberry dipped in white chocolate, albeit way less appetizing. At times, it felt as if I'd forgotten how to breathe.

That day was no exception.

It became the experience my mind immediately latched onto for years whenever I heard the word "presentation." Public speaking was pure torture. Between the relief I experienced thinking I'd been given a pass and the crushing disappointment that followed, my stutter went into overdrive. Somewhere during the walk to the front of the class, my mouth turned into a sputtering machine gun. One moment, I was talking a mile a minute, trying to get the punishment over with as quickly as possible, and the next, my mouth froze open for what felt like hours as I got hung up on words.

To make matters worse, it was the last class of the day on a Friday afternoon. In the end, my presentation ate into my classmates' weekend plans, as it took me eighteen minutes to finish my ten-minute talk. As they sprinted toward the door once I was done, I heard students say to each other, "I better not have missed my bus!"

REMEMBER THE GOOD

I wish I could say that moment and countless others like it throughout high school and college motivated me to improve my communication skills outside of working with a speech therapist. But they didn't. I'd be so relieved when I was done giving a talk that I'd celebrate by doing my best to forget about it. The only problem was that I couldn't. As the experiences stacked, the more they gnawed at me.

But it wasn't just presentations. Anything that involved a spotlight in my direction like job interviews or the mere prospect of having to converse with a stranger on the street sent a bolt of anxiety through me. It felt like the outside world paused and all eyes turned on me whenever I got stuck on a word. I hated that. I was convinced people around me were constantly saying to themselves, "What's wrong with that kid?" I despised the idea of going through life and being terrified to express myself. I constantly replayed what I should have said and how I should have said it in my head. I knew I wouldn't be able to sneak by when working in the real world, as it wasn't a secret that talking was important to getting anything done in life.

When people tell me that taking a sales job as a shy, stuttering kid was courageous, I tend to agree, but I also make a slight correction. It wasn't like I was born, stuttered for twenty-three years, and then decided one day to take a sales job. A lot of experiences took place in between. Toward the end of college and before pursuing sales, I received a few pieces of practical and actionable advice that opened my eyes to the fact that I didn't need to give a flawless presentation to a group of my peers to improve my communication skills. I learned there are countless ways to advance this skill without leaving the house or in some cases, not having to physically say a word at all.

I doubt I'll ever consider myself an expert in anything. I view myself as a curious learner and hope I always do. However, if I were to embrace a single expert identity, it would be this: focusing on the essential behind-the-scenes work to prevent feeling overwhelmed with anxiety or fear of failure when stepping into the spotlight.

I still get nervous when speaking in public or even teaching a class. Today, I'm thankful for that. It means I care. And my way of showing I care is by over-preparing and choosing to show up. Knowing what I'm talking about and not having to worry about what I'm going to say doesn't always mean things go well, but it increases the odds. After doing it so many times, even though there are nerves, there's also a tinge of excitement. The buzz of when things are going well outweighs the discomfort of getting hung up. I fight like hell to focus on words my mom repeatedly told me growing up, "Remember the good."

Some people have no problem expressing themselves. Some lunatics even enjoy public speaking. For many of us, however, it's a challenge. This is especially true if we struggle the first few times when giving presentations, bomb an interview, or leave a less than stellar first impression when meeting someone new, as those memories tend to get ingrained deeply in our heads. The only way I've discovered to overcome those memories is by practicing and choosing to make new ones. Today, when I give a talk or teach a class that most people would deem average, I celebrate as if I'd just received a standing ovation or netted a million views on a YouTube video. Through these experiences, I've developed a cheat sheet that has allowed me to slowly build the confidence to face difficult tasks, even when feeling shaky.

When I began my career, the fear of missing out on building connections with people and living life on my terms served as my primary motivators. That's still true today. However, my primary driver now is to leave a mark.

WRITE BEFORE YOU SPEAK

Before graduating from college, I went on a slew of interviews for internships and met with companies at job fairs. These interactions didn't go well. When my peers left feeling excited about the potential opportunity, I walked out thrilled it was over. One experience was especially painful. Halfway through an interview, I was asked to sell the interviewer my pen. I completely froze. I had no idea how to respond. I can still see the confused look on the interviewer's face when I stood up, handed him my pen, and stuttered my way through telling him he could have it before excusing myself from the interview. I can also still hear my roommates' laughter when I told them what had happened and I wouldn't be joining the management trainee program at Enterprise Rent-A-Car.

My confidence began to rise when I met with a career coach. "It's amazing that people spend a fortune on an education only to blow the end-game by not investing a couple of hundred dollars in their interview skills," he told me as he sold me. "Not only does learning how to successfully navigate interviews allow you to potentially earn hundreds of thousands of additional dollars throughout the duration of your career, but the confidence of making the effort rolls over into other aspects of your life."

I hated hearing this, but the man was absolutely right. If you prioritize improving your interview skills, it helps you to get more comfortable with people on the street as well as speaking in front of groups. The confidence you gain by doing the work to navigate potentially stressful situations reduces the nerves in your run-of-the-mill interactions. Rather than diving into voicing my answers to typical interview questions, just like my speech therapist advised in Principle 2, my career coach demanded that I pick up a pen. Over the following months, I had to write out my answers word for word for the twenty most common questions I'd most likely be asked in interviews for us to discuss and rip apart when we met.

This may sound like a chore and not how you want to spend your free time, but regardless of whether you enjoy writing, it's crucial. The words "writing is thinking," are cliché for a reason; they're grounded in truth. Life is about pattern recognition. Few things expedite this process faster than taking the time to get curious on paper. Writing our ideas, our stories, our wins and losses, or even just our random thoughts allows us to better connect the dots we've collected. But I'd take the notion that writing is thinking one step further by adding it is the single best way to improve our verbal communication skills. It allows us to think before we speak and helps us to cut down on the worry of *what* we're going to say, leaving us to focus solely on *how* we're going to say it.

When beginning this exercise of chipping away at interview questions, your answers don't have to be perfect. That comes with practice. Discovering yourself and honing your communication skills is forever work. The important thing is to start. If beginning with interview questions feels like homework, choose something that sounds fun. Write down your favorite stories, take notes on a book you are reading, anything and everything you can think of to get that business idea off the ground or steal any of the thousands of journaling prompts available online. You can even begin by writing about your public speaking fears or how much you hate interviews. Getting your big fears written down in little words doesn't automatically mean the problem is half solved, but it helps. One thing I like to do each day is to write a few sentences regarding the following five questions:

- What's one thing I learned today?
- What's one memory I thought about?
- What's one thing I'm proud of?
- What's one thing I could have done better?
- What's one way someone helped me?

This should be the only homework assignment we're given in school. The beauty of these questions is the longer you stick with them, the more they will teach you how to see—which is arguably the most important life skill that very few people talk about.

You will naturally look for learning opportunities from your past and present, areas where you can improve, the good in others, and the good inside yourself. You may find that thanks to these answers you feel more confident in interviews, preparing for presentations, and conversations on the street, as you've begun to collect stories of your highs and lows and the lessons you've learned along the way. Essentially, these questions are a cheat sheet to continually raise your self-awareness. If they resonate, steal these questions. Or better yet, create your own list of daily prompts to ponder that are more in line with what you're looking to achieve. The question alone of noting the things you're proud of has the power to reframe the story you tell yourself regarding your worth. Confidence isn't only found by accomplishing your big goals. It's also found by consistently doing what you feel is right. Rather than look for outside validation, track the good you do and validate yourself.

Despite having a severe stutter, whenever I take the time to write before I speak, I stutter much less and I rarely hesitate to speak up if I have something to say. At first, this surprised me. But it makes perfect sense: I no longer worry about what I'm going to say, I simply have to focus on saying something I've already written.

OBSERVE BEFORE YOU SPEAK

I got lucky in college. I had an extremely empathetic political science teacher, Mr. Kitchen. Recognizing my fear and discomfort when having to speak in class, he gave me two pieces of advice. First, he encouraged me when possible to not wait to be called on and to suck it up and go first. He reinforced the notion my speech therapist shared that it would free up the headspace to listen to other people instead of freaking out about how much I'd potentially screw up when it was my turn to talk. Second, he encouraged me to be a keen observer of the presentations of my classmates. He told me to keep track of what they did well, whether or not they got my attention in their introduction, and how much I was persuaded to support their argument.

I wish I could say I immediately turned his suggestions into action. At times, I still hesitated to volunteer and I still got stuck in my head imagining all the bad things that would happen when being called upon. When I did follow his advice—and I took notes on not only the content of the presentations of my peers but also their delivery—over time, it sent me down a rabbit hole to better understand what strong communication looked like.

This act of observation, however, goes way past presentations. The world is a classroom. Every day, we have countless opportunities to study effective communicators in an array of situations from meetings at work and water cooler chats to encounters on the street and dinner parties. How do people approach each other? What do they say as icebreakers? Are there any questions they ask that open up the conversation to discuss in more detail certain aspects of someone's experiences? When we think they could have done something better, we discover ways to say it more effectively, which we can apply to our own communication when facing similar situations.

As this habit compounded, I essentially created a database of what attracts human beings to each other and what doesn't. I became more present. The mindset shift of thinking "What can I learn today?" is much more productive than saying to ourselves, "I'll never be able to do that!"

The best part of committing to observe the communication of others is it doesn't involve speaking at all. There's absolutely nothing wrong with choosing the easy path when approaching a difficult task. The purpose of observing others isn't just to exactly mirror the words and actions but rather note the aspects that appeal to you, feel natural to you, and enlarge the true you. The only expert label that matters is that of being yourself.

DISSECT BEFORE YOU SPEAK

The benefit of being more intentional with observing the communication of other people is that over time it opens the door to better dissecting their communication. Today, in addition to our peers, we have countless online resources at our fingertips to learn from. But for starters, zero in on people's introductions when watching talks, because if you nail that, the rest becomes easier as momentum is your friend. Pay close attention to which tactics speakers use to hook us, whether it's through a story, an engaging question, or a thought-provoking statement. As speakers advance through their talk, we can dissect the phrases they use to transition from point to point as well as how they use the power of pausing at certain times to better drive home an idea. In addition, we can dive into their use of metaphors, analogies, and imagery to simplify complicated ideas, and how they conclude their talk to inspire others to take action or to see the world through a new lens.

The learning you'll accumulate by dissecting just one TED Talk a week will astound you. The speakers are sharing a theory, idea, or strongly held belief, and they have eighteen minutes to persuade us. Comparing the effectiveness of these talks will give you a crash course on how to structure your own stories and arguments.

My favorite platform for dissection is *The Moth*. It contains countless videos of people sharing personal stories that feel very real and very raw, like an old friend sharing their honest experience in an intimate setting. One of the patterns you'll notice in these stories is that rather than share an experience that demonstrates how amazing the speakers are, they tell stories that are rooted in struggle. In its purest form, this is what a story is—the recounting of a character navigating a challenge. They take you on a journey from point A to point B while sharing the bruises and triumphs they collected along the way. When done well, this creates a hard-to-resist mix of someone being brave enough to face a challenge and vulnerable enough to open themselves up to their missteps and misfires.

This should give you great confidence. You don't need to have life figured out to tell a great story. If you've failed a bunch or if you've experienced fear, uncertainty, doubt, or embarrassment, you're sitting on a potential gold mine as these emotions define the human experience and allow others to know they aren't alone.

We can also dissect communication by listening to podcasts. While we may look forward to hearing a big-name guest's story, there's a lot to be learned from the host as well. How do they frame their questions and guide their conversations in a way that allows their guests to reveal themselves? Upon receiving an answer, rather than move on to the next question, many of the best hosts use these phrases: "I'm curious . . ." "I'm interested . . . " "Back to your point about . . ." To ensure the interview doesn't feel like a Q&A, they play conversation ping-pong by sharing their own perspectives and stories sparked by the guest's answers. Similar to the mindset of a "trampoline" discussed in Principle 2, by interjecting their own experiences and perspectives, the host bounces ideas and stories back to enlarge both the guest and the conversation.

Before developing this obsession, when watching strong communicators, my internal dialog was in the gutter. I berated myself while comparing their practiced product to my non-practiced product. Over time, however, my self-talk got curious. Rather than beating myself up for not being as polished, I made a commitment to practice. Sure, some people may come from a stronger starting line. But no one is born with a microphone in their hand. The more effortless strong communication looks, the more effort someone puts into it. Thanks to technology and assuming we don't live in a cave, every day we have countless opportunities to improve our communication skills by observing and dissecting the communication of others.

RECORD YOURSELF SPEAKING

During the pandemic, Kelly Corrigan, the host of the PBS show *Tell Me More*, asked me to join her on her podcast *Kelly Corrigan Wonders* to talk about how my wife and I met and "what attracts." I was over the moon. I'd just listened to Kelly interview Margaret Atwood, the author of the best-selling book *The Handmaid's Tale*, a few weeks prior.

Not an hour after I received Kelly's invitation, however, I received another message. Only this time, I learned a loved one had been diagnosed with a serious health issue. Since I couldn't travel back to the United States due to quarantine to be with them, I felt paralyzed. On top of this, the test results that would either confirm the gravity of the initial prognosis or add a ray of light to the situation were scheduled for the very day I was supposed to record with Kelly. Being that bad news tends to travel in threes, I also learned that, prior to recording, I was to read two articles out loud in their entirety on the podcast. This may not sound like a big deal. But for me, reading out loud is akin to being asked to eat nails. It's something I continually struggle with to this day, as I stutter much more than normal when reading out loud in front of people.

Knowing that my loved one's response would be to not cancel the interview and give it everything I had, I leaned into every trick I knew to gain a semblance of control and raise my confidence levels. In addition to rewriting the articles multiple times to have them fresh in my head, I dissected countless videos and sought out advice from strong speakers I know like my friend Nick Wolny. Nick is a beyond-talented writer and teacher who regularly appears as a guest on mainstream platforms including CBS, FOX, and NBC to discuss emerging trends in the creator economy. Per his advice, to get in additional reps, I found ways to incorporate speaking in public into my average days. I recruited a few friends to trade stories with over Zoom, got even more intentional when reading bedtime stories at night to my kids, and volunteered to read stories at my kids' school. The logic? If I could keep the attention of a group of three-year-olds, adults would be a breeze. Most of all, however, to prepare for the interview, I leaned into my go-to tactic of recording myself discussing questions I thought Kelly might ask as well as the stories I was tasked with reading.

I'm convinced that if you commit to writing and recording yourself talking about what you've written, it isn't a matter of *if* your career takes off, but *when*. The key to career success is to have an "and." The world is full of strong coders, designers, and engineers. The ones that stand out, however, are more than one-dimensional. Someone who is a strong coder "and" gives engaging presentations wins more opportunities than someone who doesn't. Put simply, your "and" is your X factor. The fastest way to create this edge is by prioritizing your communication skills as they amplify your technical skills.

When doing this exercise, start with audio only. This will allow you to focus solely on the content and your tone and pace instead of worrying about how you look. You can begin by reading your notes while slowly relying less and less on the script. It's always good to get feedback from other people, but with this exercise, you'll know a handful of the things you could have done better, as we're our own worst critic. Pay attention to the times you got tripped up as well as the times you got something right. Do it again the next day. Then again. You'll be shocked by how much you are improving after just a few takes. You'll begin to see which words you use as a crutch like "umm" or "like." You'll also see where you rushed things and could have benefited from a pause to better drive a point home. Additionally, as you transition to include video, you'll see how you're maintaining eye contact and what messages your body language is sending.

The point of taking note of the things you got right is crucial. As humans, we tend to focus on our mistakes and easily forget about the good we do. Momentum, however, is created by building on areas of competence and confidence. So yes, identify ways for improvement. But don't forget to take the time to recognize the aspects you got right.

Grab the twenty most common interview questions you've written your answers for and record yourself answering just one a day. Move on to telling your favorite stories and take what you've learned by watching talks and make the necessary adjustments so your introduction is engaging. By doing this one exercise every day for a few minutes, combined with physically taking the time to write, you may be surprised by not just how much your communication will improve but also how much your confidence will rise.

I wish I could say the interview with Kelly went off without a hitch by doing all this work. But it wasn't my best day. I got tripped up in a few places and due to the circumstances of waiting for my loved one's test results, my voice had a lot less energy than it normally does. A month later, however, I got a chance to redeem myself. I was asked to give a thirty-minute talk regarding how to grow an engaged audience on the online writing platform *Medium* in front of a group of well-known authors. Darius Foroux, one of my favorite people in the creator space, along with a dozen others, messaged me afterward saying how inspiring my talk had been.

Be in Awe of People

I don't know where I'd be if a few good people hadn't passed on a few pieces of practical advice that got me curious about ways to improve my communication that didn't feel overwhelming. Today, when moving to a new town and needing to make new friends or when teaching a new class, the connections I make form quickly. I'd even go so far as to say building connections with others is my strongest skill which is a far cry from that scared, sputtering kid who once made his classmates stay eight minutes after class during eleventh-grade history class.

The beauty of these suggestions is you're probably already writing in some form or another, observing other people's conversations, watching videos, and tinkering with your phone. These exercises are about being more intentional with how you're using these tools and embracing technology as a force for betterment.

In the process of studying other people and making a commitment to improving our own communication skills, rather than comparing ourselves to others, our eyes can open to how incredible people are. Kevin Ervin Kelley, a man whose genius you're going to learn more about in the next chapter and who makes his living designing spaces that bring people together, summed up perhaps the best communication advice that exists. "Some people experience awe visiting the Grand Canyon or watching a sunset in Maui. I experience awe watching everyday humans going about their everyday lives."

I don't know about you, but I love that. It serves as a powerful reminder that we will never have a dull life if we adopt the mind-set of viewing people as endlessly fascinating.

By making a commitment to treat our curiosity as our primary responsibility and putting in the work to better express ourselves on our own terms, over time, we'll not only create more connections with others, but we'll build more meaningful ones.

PART II
MEANINGFUL CONNECTIONS

Principle 5

Get to Know Your Heroes

Kevin Ervin Kelly is the author of the book *Irreplaceable*, cofounder of the bicoastal strategy design firm Shook Kelley, and my frequent writing partner. When he was twenty-eight years old, he did something that everyone thought was not only absurd but reckless.

Kevin was buried in student debt with a young child to support. On top of this situation, he and his (now) longtime business partner had just launched their firm. Like most new businesses, they were paying out more money than they were bringing in. Despite the circumstances, after seeing a brochure for a postgraduate summer course in design, marketing, and branding at Harvard University several times, Kevin said to hell with it and cut a check he prayed wouldn't bounce to attend the course.

Why was he dead set on making this investment? The instructor was none other than his idol, legendary architect Gene Kohn, whose firm KPF has helped define our modern-day city skyline across the globe. Kevin knew if he wanted to make an impact, he'd need to get to know the people who were already making one.

His family, team members, and cofounder were not happy when they heard about his decision. "It's not the time!" they told him. "You're already underwater. Harvard can wait!" Not only that, but the renowned Ivy League institution was a different world from the swamps of South Florida, where Kevin grew up. No matter the pushback or his parents' echoes in the back of his mind that reminded him, "Never get too far above your raising," Kevin took the leap, anyway.

A few months later, though, as soon as he stepped foot on the campus to begin the course, doubts flooded his head. "Maybe they're right!" he mentally berated himself. "Maybe I don't belong here!" To make matters worse, on his first day of class, every head in the room turned as his boot-cut jeans and red flannel shirt clashed against a sea of khaki pants and tweed jackets. As Kevin scanned the room and met eyes with people twice his age and ten times his experience, his worries went into overdrive. He questioned if he'd just thrown a large sum of tuition money out the window.

Once Gene Kohn walked through the door, however, Kevin settled in and committed to sit quietly at the back of the class and learn as much as he could from the man he'd read so much about in books and magazines. Kevin's patience paid off on the second day of class when Mr. Kohn did something surprising. Before the course began, students were tasked with submitting a project. Rifling through a stack of them, Mr. Kohn picked one up and asked, "Whose work is this?"

Sheepishly, Kevin replied, "Mine, sir." He'd been convinced the work he'd created wasn't up to par or that he'd broken the submission guidelines of the historied institution. But much to his amazement, Mr. Kohn instead asked him if he'd be up for talking about his work, process, and approach.

For the next hour, Kevin did just that. His initial nervousness turned to confidence as the class hung on his every word. As they took copious notes, Kevin walked them through his project and answered question after question while laying out human behavior principles that had been influential to his work.

The surprises from Mr. Kohn didn't end there. Taken aback by the young student, he pulled Kevin aside after class and asked him if he'd be up for having lunch the following day.

Twenty-four hours later, Kevin found himself one on one with his idol. According to Kevin, it was the most stimulating conversation he'd ever had as the two men shared war stories and theories on the future of design. While waiting for the check, Mr. Kohn offered up one last question. It became a question that would ultimately change the course of Kevin's life forever. "What do you think about teaching this course next year with me?"

Despite being half the age of most of the students and not having any previous teaching experience, for eleven years Kevin taught design, marketing, and branding alongside his idol. Because he treated curiosity as his primary responsibility, it allowed his career to career into the stratosphere. Mr. Kohn was not only generous with his time and knowledge but also with his network. He introduced Kevin to influential figure after influential figure. Most importantly, Kevin discovered a lifelong mentor and advisor in Mr. Kohn, and up until Gene's passing in early 2023, the two remained close friends.

If you were to ask Kevin how it all came to fruition, he'd first acknowledge a little bit of luck and a solid slice of privilege to have the opportunity to get in front of Mr. Kohn. Then he'd tell you in his often intense, smokey southern drawl, it's because he followed his nose and took the risk of turning his hero into a friend.

How a Nobody Becomes Somebody (By Contacting Other Somebodies)

Close to thirty years have passed since Kevin ignored the advice of his peers and went to a place "he had no business being in." But his eagerness to get to know people he was curious about didn't stop there nor did it start there.

Each week, dating as far back as high school, Kevin would sit down and write a handwritten letter to someone he admired either in the architecture and design space, business world, or human behavior or culture lanes. It's a practice, despite the way communication has changed, that he still exercises today.

Mapping out letters to build relationships with those he admired took time, not solely from the effort to write a note, but also in conducting the research. It's gotten easier as his career has advanced and his knowledge, network, and experiences have compounded. In the early days, however, he had to master the art of not only piquing someone's interest but also crafting his message in a way that kept their attention and earned a conversation.

Looking back, Kevin estimates his early success rate of a reply barely scraped 5 percent. The reason he kept at it is fourfold.

- First, sitting down to write a letter helped sharpen his thinking and form theories on the market and where our culture was heading. This is something he advises we all do no matter what sector we're in.

- Second, it forced him to dig a layer deeper into the stories and thought processes of the people he was reaching out to, to ask questions that weren't easily answered elsewhere.

- Third, even if they didn't reply, it got his name in front of them in a memorable fashion. Handwritten letters are hard to dismiss without reading them first.

- Last, the 5 percent that *did* reply made all the difference and more than made up for the 95 percent that didn't reply.

Because of his outreach messages, he built relationships with CEOs of the largest banks in the United States. He connected with renowned designers, global thought leaders, and authors of books he liked. Put together, these relationships have played a key role in helping Kevin's firm stay afloat for over three decades without ever having a marketing department in an environment where businesses fail faster than most influencers upload TikTok videos.

True to form, I met Kevin when he personally reached out. Over the years, he'd learned how to sell and communicate effectively in person, but he wanted to improve his writing skills. His goal was to adapt to the new world of less formal, yet more conversational language so his message would hit a broader audience. His initial email stated, "When learning something new, I seek out the best. And in my eyes, you're that and I have many articles of yours printed out on my desk as a reminder of what clear, concise, and most of all, memorable writing looks like." The guy knows how to sell, doesn't he?

Today, I couldn't imagine my life without Kevin. He's a quick study. Similar to how he moved from student to teacher at Harvard, today he helps me with my writing just as much as I assist him. To continually scratch each other's backs, I'll occasionally jump in on a branding project for one of his clients while he gives guest lectures for my students about how to get a seat at the leadership table.

Of all the stories I've heard about people carving their own path because they've been curious about other people, I've highlighted Kevin's experience for two reasons. First, even though it's a big example of what's possible, it shows that anything is indeed possible. Second, Kevin conducted his outreach on his terms. He leaned into his strength of being a nonstop reader, asking good questions, and seeking out the teachers he wanted to learn from.

To this day, Kevin still writes handwritten letters once or twice a month. Naturally, this takes time, but changing the medium to something more personal than a social media message shifts people's context. Think about that for a moment. What would you do if you received a sincere and curious letter from someone? Especially if they were just starting in their career? Perhaps you wouldn't reply in the same format, but the odds are high that you'd at least read it, right?

To emphasize just how powerful this method is, while I was writing this book, Kaki Okumora, the twenty-three-year-old author of the beautiful and impactful book, *Wa: The Art of Balance*, sent me a letter on traditional Japanese paper. Her letter included two hand-drawn postcards that accompanied a message expressing appreciation for my support. I immediately sent her a message back. But first, I showed my wife and then asked my kids to hang the beautiful letter on our fridge. Even though this practice takes additional effort, both Kaki and Kevin save time because they've carved out reputations rooted in thoughtfulness—a priceless quality no amount of money can buy.

HIT THE SEND BUTTON

Shortly after I began writing, I took a similar approach to Kevin's personalized notes. I committed each week to reach out to one writer I admired whose work resonated, with the hopes of getting them on a call to learn more about them. Despite my background in sales, the fear of sending these messages was on another level. In sales, if things go south over the phone, I'd never hear from that person again. However, reaching out to people who were doing what I wanted to do meant they'd likely read some of my work before deciding if I was worth their time, which opened the door to judgment and rejection. I didn't have a large following either when I began this practice. I had roughly five hundred followers on the writing platform *Medium* and wasn't active on other social media platforms. Essentially, I was a nobody in the online world.

The reason I did it was simple: I'd fallen in love with writing and I wanted to get to know people who were better at it than I was. Within a year, I improved *what* I was doing to the point I could support my family from my writing alone, all because I chose to prioritize *who* I was meeting. In early conversations, an initial bond was formed over our shared passion for writing. But as these relationships progressed, our conversations expanded past our work which is where friendships were forged. The people I connected with introduced me to other writers they knew, and as my network grew, I did the same for them.

Seven Steps to Turn Your Heroes into Friends

It can be hard to ignore the idea that we have to be successful and have our lives together to be noticed by people we deem to operate at a high level. If I've learned anything through my experience, it's that being a curious learner and attentive observer is just as attractive, if not more so, than being an "expert."

When we pursue a field that excites us or when we even engage in activities such as a side hustle or a hobby, our enthusiasm can be our greatest strength. The right people not only respect that but can relate to it. When Kevin began rubbing shoulders with industry titans, several friends asked how he did it. He said:

> There are two things about successful people most people don't realize. First, they're surrounded by impressive people all day every day. Trying to impress them by acting like you know all the answers is a surefire way for them to walk right past you. Second, the right ones love to teach and share their wisdom. I was able to become part of their circle because I positioned myself as a sponge and soaked up every lesson they imparted to me. A mindset that I still lead with today.

Kevin's advice rings true. While I'm partial to getting in front of people face to face and being out and about in the real world, technology has made us a globalized world. The barriers to connecting with people haven't evaporated entirely. But thanks to email and social media, they've been seriously lowered, making the ability to craft messages that net a response an extremely valuable skill.

During the last six years, I've reached out to over three hundred people ranging from writers half my age whose style and message I like, to industry leaders thirty years my senior. Sometimes I reach out to people from a polar opposite array of fields whose work attracts my attention. Through this experience and testing out different ways to get in front of people, some patterns have emerged regarding what's worked well and what hasn't been as effective.

The eight points below form a cheat sheet full of tips and tactics to turn heroes into friends. You'll notice I don't ask for much—if anything at all—when first reaching out as my initial goal is simply to open a line of communication. The following chapter, "Friendships Are Forged in the Follow-Up," serves as an extension of this chapter and will dive deeper into how to advance these relationships.

1. Pick One Platform, and Limit Your Outreach to One Person a Week (or Month)

Although email is frowned upon and gets a lot of heat from people, I love it. The reason is threefold.

- First, picking one means of primary communication keeps you organized.
- Second, most people have their email open all day.
- Last, most messages in people's inboxes steal energy whereas sending an appreciative message stands out.

My rationale for once a week also comes down to organization. On any given day, dozens of people come into our orbit on social media. Choosing one person to dig into reduces the noise and provides the space to dive deeper into their experiences. This practice will also build your confidence because you're doing the necessary prep work and will feel prepared as opposed to nervous or intimidated.

If one person a week sounds like a lot, then there's nothing wrong with moving slowly and aiming to connect with one person each month. The important thing is to keep moving. Making one solid contact a month adds up over time. Contrary to conventional wisdom, we don't need a massive network to make an impact. We need a supportive one.

2. Start Smart by Starting Small

"Inside every apartment building you walk by on any given day are interesting people doing interesting things." My mom told me this years ago. She followed up that sage advice with another zinger: "If you find one person interesting, everyone is interesting." I'll never forget her words. It's easy to get wrapped up in the idea we need someone like Oprah, Bill Gates, or Elon Musk to give us our big break. A much easier strategy, however, is to find like-minded people you enjoy sharing ideas and stories with. Though a good practice to test your skills as you never know what may come from it, the odds of a household name opening their front door for you to "pick their brain" are slim.

Instead, start smart by identifying friends of friends who are doing cool things, or reach out to other people who've mentioned they share similar interests and habits. The point is to start where you're comfortable. People like Kevin hold their own with the Gene Kohns of the world because he'd spent a decade reaching out to other fascinating people. Once the opportunity presented itself, he'd had enough practice and didn't feel like he was playing in a foreign league.

The key to any new habit is collecting easy wins to build momentum. One connection has a funny way of turning into two. An important reminder, though. Never—*ever*—view the people you initially reach out to as stepping stones to get to know someone "more important." The entire point of getting to know people is to identify if you're a good match to grow together and not to use them like you would a rung on the ladder of success.

3. Know Your North Star

When I first became serious about writing, I was encouraged to put the following question at the top of each draft to ensure

I stayed on point: "After reading this, I want the reader to _____?"

You can apply this same strategy to writing your outreach message. Have one clear agenda. Whether it's to show appreciation for their work, ask their take on a question, or inspire them to get on a call with you, make sure your goal is clear. Your message should support exactly what you're looking to accomplish and nothing more. Too many requests or questions often lead to little or no response because the message can appear pushy, scattered, or flat-out overwhelming.

Think about the type of messages you'd reply to from a stranger. The odds are high they wouldn't include having to search for their point or struggle to identify how to respond or best support them. This simple act of asking yourself, "Why am I reaching out to this person?" and being honest in the response allows you to gauge if you truly are curious about the person or view them solely as a way to get ahead.

4. Embrace the "Rule of 7"

One of the oldest principles in marketing is the "Rule of 7," which states that a prospective customer needs to be exposed to an advertiser's message seven times before they'll take action. This doesn't mean that if you send an email and don't get a response, you should follow up six more times (please don't do that). However, it *does* mean that a person will be more apt to open an email from you if they're familiar with your name.

Most of us are tired of feeling like just another name in a sea of people trying to make connections online. The key to standing out is to be strategic about how you get your name in front of others. Instead of jumping straight to direct contact, consider indirect approaches that pique their interest and build familiarity. Sharing their work on social media with a brief comment about how it impacted you is one way. If you have a blog, you can write a post that mentions how their work has positively affected you, then tag them on X or LinkedIn, thanking them for the inspiration. This shows both thoughtfulness and effort. If TikTok videos are your thing, use this social aspect in a way to catch their attention or simply engage with their posts. Get creative. The likelihood of receiving a positive response to any request is higher if you do this beforehand. The point is to find an avenue of approach that's the least uncomfortable for you to begin to get in front of them. Just don't do too many things at once, too close together, or you'll risk turning them off.

The very first comment I left online before I even began writing was under a blog post for Steven Pressfield, author of numerous bestsellers including *The Legend of Bagger Vance* and *The War of Art*. The next day, his team reached out to ask if they could use my comment in a future article they were preparing on how to network and pitch yourself. "Of course," I replied before sharing another tip that had worked well for me in my response which was also included in the article. More recently, another writer I admire, Amy Shearn, author of *Unseen City*, asked her audience on X for ways people pleasers can get more comfortable saying no. Shortly thereafter, she reached out to thank me for offering a suggestion and to let me know my response was included in an article she wrote for *Oprah Magazine*. In both instances, I was just sharing something I'd learned and other people deemed the advice valuable, which opened the door for a potential conversation.

5. Craft an Authentic, Yet Compelling Subject Line

Once you've completed the first four steps, it's time to write your email. This includes crafting a compelling subject line that persuades them to open a message from someone on the outskirts of their immediate network.

The subject line "Friend of [mutual friend's name]" can be extremely effective assuming you have a common connection as it's a hard subject line to ignore. But there are a lot of solid options that are hard to dismiss. Your job is to find one that feels authentic to you. In one experiment, entrepreneur and author Shane Snow found that simple subject lines like "Quick question" net strong results when reaching out to new people.[1] Marketers, however, are starting to use this subject line more often, so its effectiveness might be waning. Plus, if you use this tactic, your question *better* be quick and not an answer you can easily Google.

In my experience, the subject line "Thank you" has consistently been the most effective in starting conversations, or a variation like "A note of appreciation for your work." This may sound basic, but the effectiveness of this subject line may surprise you. As implied previously, it stands out because most inboxes tend *not* to be filled with thank-you messages. It also leads to the next point which begins the body of the outreach message.

6. Show Them What Their Work Has Helped You Achieve

Everyone, regardless of their background, appreciates the feeling that their work is meaningful and is making a positive impact. Once you have a solid subject line, consider applying this formula to your message: "Thanks to you doing X, I've been able to achieve Y." But don't take the easy route here with a general compliment. Instead, get specific about their work, such as a particular story, idea, or system they shared, and then explain how it has helped you achieve a desired outcome. The outcome could be something like landing an interview or creating a successful presentation.

Why is this tactic so effective? It shows you're putting their work into practice. You can even begin your outreach by asking for their one tip to improve a skill and once you've implemented it, report back your findings and specify how it helped you. Most people have a soft spot for those who value their advice and are geared to take action.

Here's a sample format to steal:

Hello, Rachel. As a longtime reader, I wanted to let you know your advice about how to navigate the interview question of "Tell me about yourself" is golden. I used it just last week and by confidently answering it, the rest of the interview went swimmingly (sorry, my mom loves that word). I just learned I landed a second interview. No need to reply but thanks again for doing what you do. It helps. Best to you and yours, Michael

Inside this note are a few things worth noticing. First, dropping in an odd word like "swimmingly" and referencing my mom may sound odd, but it humanizes me. Second, the words "no need to reply" can often net a reply. (It works similar to one of those reverse psychology things where you state: "I'm not sure this is for you . . ." only to have most people get curious why it's not for them.)

7. Don't Underestimate Your Ability to Make Their Life Easier or More Enjoyable

Successful people are often busy. This makes it an easy excuse for us to tell ourselves it's a waste of time contacting them. But here's the thing: if they're busy, they may need help. If you can identify a challenge they're facing and position yourself as a potential antidote to said challenge, they might become open to getting to know you.

Coming up with a way to help someone who on the outside looks like they don't need any assistance may sound complicated. But if you learn to read between the lines and glean information from their social media accounts, you'll discover little clues littered throughout their online presence about what they're up to or working on.

Here are some examples:

- "I'm launching a new product" is code for "I could use some help spreading the word."

- "I'm really excited about starting a podcast" is code for "Does anyone have any experience with this?"
- "I'm moving to Barcelona" is code for "Does anybody have any connections or recommendations in that part of the world?"
- "I'm stoked that my book is coming out soon" is code for "I could use some help with the launch to ensure people buy it."

Clues to making real connections online are everywhere. Your job is to learn how to spot them and present your solution in an easily digestible manner.

Here's how to craft a basic outline for an effective outreach message:

- Thank the person for the work they do and how it's specifically helped you.
- Point out an aspect of their work you may be able to help them with.
- Provide a few ideas on how you could get involved to make their life easier or better.

And here's how this might look in draft form:

Hello, Rachel. Thank you for the work you're doing on mindfulness for people with ADHD. I often beat myself up for not being able to meditate first thing in the morning. That one sentence you wrote—"consider exercising first thing to burn some energy and then meditate once your mind has settled"—has been life-changing. For the first time, I've finally been able to reap the rewards of meditation. I noticed in your recent newsletter that you're making a push for your new book. I'd be happy to get involved to spread the word or help organize a launch team. If that interests you, below are a few ideas.

[Insert two or three bullet points]. If not, no worries. As my uncle says, "receiving a no beats not knowing." Thank you for doing what you do. It's helpful. I can't wait to read your book. Best to you and yours, Michael.

Shortly after moving to Barcelona, I cleaned up the copy on the websites of a few Spanish entrepreneurs whose sites were in English and I sent over the edits for free. I didn't have professional writing or editing experience but as a native English speaker, I knew I could help. A client caught wind of this and referred me to her friend, Albert Moreno, who was looking to build a website in English. Albert and I hit it off immediately. So much so that he asked me to join his startup, and after working together for a year, he offered me ownership and for three years we worked hand in hand to expand into international markets.

The beauty of this message is that it shows you're willing to do the very kind of work that's beneficial to the person you're contacting and you've put some thought into it. This makes it easy for you to stand out among all the other people asking for something without first offering—or in the best cases—giving something of value.

Is this time-consuming? Absolutely. But so is anything worth having. Plus, I don't know about you but I'd rather hunt for the people I want to work for and put some thought into how to make a stand-out impression rather than apply for random jobs online. Put yourself in the shoes of the person you admire, and ask yourself: Who would impress me more? Someone who went deep or someone who barely scratched past surface level?

8. Never Underestimate the Power of Quirks
Famed furniture designer Charles Eames famously said, "The details aren't the details, the details are the thing." When researching someone, keep this in mind and train your eyes to see what

others miss. Doing so gets people's attention and often, the response of, "How'd you uncover that!" nets positive results.

When researching a talented American food, travel, and culture writer based in Barcelona, I discovered that he adores a type of bread he once had in Southern Spain that reminded him of English muffins from the United States. With the sort of resume the man had, I opted not to go hard at him for writing advice. Instead, I simply shared the following:

> I'm a big fan of your work. I read that you have a thing for a certain type of bread in Malaga that reminds you of English Muffins. I live in Vic [a town in Spain I was living in at the time] and a corner store I go to may have what you're looking for as the first thing I thought when I tried it was, "My God, this is like a massive English Muffin." I'd be happy to drop off a few rounds the next time I'm in Barcelona. Take care, Michael

Shortly thereafter, I received a message saying they'd love to meet up and they were eager to see how the bread stacked up. Because of COVID-19 and life getting in the way, the man has since moved back to the United States. Still, he was kind enough to hop on a call and give me some pointers about navigating book publishers and reinforced the importance of following my nose on the topic I wanted to explore. In sum, details matter. The more specific the better, as it shows you've dug deeper than the average duck.

IGNORE CONVENTIONAL WISDOM AND EVERYTHING I JUST SAID

The world is full of advice regarding how to build relationships with people you admire. I prefer to use email as the initial contact. Maybe for you, it's direct messages on X or LinkedIn. I try to keep my messages to four sentences or less. My friend Brian Pennie, however, reached out to over one hundred CEOs in his home country of Ireland with a four-paragraph message. It netted an 81 percent response rate. His achievement wasn't due to his impressive resume as Brian was a recovering heroin addict, and when doing this outreach, he was delivering food to make ends meet while studying at a local university. The combination of optimism, boldness, honesty, and a burning desire to make a positive impact on the world stood out. Inside his message, he owned his narrative and clearly expressed his goal, "to share tools from resilient and successful people to the next generation." This speaks directly to the power of identifying your north star and clarifying your "why" for contacting people that extend past your benefit. In six months, Brian met with many of the people he reached out to and ultimately was invited to lead workshops and give talks for their respective organizations. Making this effort also led to landing a book deal for his hard-to-put-down memoir *Bonus Time*.

In life, there are a million and two ways to get from zero to one. Find a way that's maybe not 100 percent comfortable, but something you feel is definitely doable. Maybe volunteering to help with events intrigues you. Playing a supportive role in an area you care about is a good way to meet like-minded people while getting in front of event organizers who often have vast networks, as well as those giving talks. Or maybe it's hosting dinner parties where you invite a handful of interesting people. My friend and past student Martin Nait built relationships with his classmates doing this very thing as he loves to cook. Perhaps for you, it's connecting with people one on one in person. If focusing online is your strength, lean into it. Most of all, if what you're doing isn't working, don't change yourself. Change your messaging and try different techniques until you find one that works.

When starting a career, feeling stuck, or looking for a change, our desire to learn can attract more people than we think. As a teacher, I encounter many project managers or individuals aspiring to become one. Although it may seem awkward to reach out to those in our desired field and believe they won't want to speak with us, my students who push past their self-doubt and actively connect with project managers at desirable companies tend to do well for themselves.

Benjamin Sledge, the award-winning author of the gripping war memoir, *Where Cowards Go to Die*, and my editor, said it best: "One good conversation can change our stars. One good friend can alter our fortune. One good mentor can give clarity to our direction."

We live in an incredible time. Never has it been easier to get on the radar of people we admire. By honing these habits you not only open the door for something you may consider impossible to become possible, but in the meantime, you'll also improve your communication as you learn to write messages where every word counts. Additionally, your confidence will also skyrocket because you've chosen to go after what you want and you'll soon realize the power of one yes. Arguably more importantly, you'll realize that the world didn't implode because of a lack of response or a rejection.

As Kevin, whose story we started this chapter with, said, "So what if they do? I say no all the time. I'm busy. So are other people. But the right people don't sit around judging people for going after what they want. Any time I get a message from someone, no matter if I have the time or not, respect is there as I know how challenging putting yourself out into the world can be."

Think deeply about *what* you want to do and *how* you're going to do it. But don't underestimate the power of *who*. Commit to doing it your way. Good things happen when we create the space to ask ourselves, "Which interesting person am I going to meet today?"

Now, let's dig into how we can turn these initial connections into friends through thoughtful follow-up.

Principle 6

Friendships Are Forged in the Follow-Up

I WAS ONCE TOLD WE LOOK TO MAKE FRIENDS WITH PEOPLE WHO possess qualities we'd like to emulate. There's a lot of truth to that. Growing up shy with a stutter, I was constantly in awe of confident, outgoing people; those who made people's heads turn when they walked into a room and seemed to connect with everyone from adults to their peers with ease. As a defense mechanism, I often hid among them as a way to feel protected and mask my own insecurities. After all, sometimes the safest place for the quietest kid to sit is behind the strongest or the loudest kids.

However beneficial—as I'm sure I unconsciously picked up on their habits and mannerisms—the learning that made the biggest impact came from observing and getting to know other people who fall on the more shy or reserved side, yet still were great with meeting new people and maintaining friendships. One childhood friend in particular, Anthony, is especially talented with this skill. Despite having four kids, being heavily involved in nonprofit initiatives over the last two decades, and having a highly successful career in financial services, he remains the glue that has held our high school friend group together. He's easily the best friendship maintainer I've ever met, and it turns out there's a reason for that: he learned early on in his career how valuable the skill is.

Anthony took an internship when he was in college at a global financial services firm. He pursued the job solely because he had no idea what he wanted to do after graduating and it was the only offer outside of spending another summer as a lifeguard at our local pool. For the duration of the internship, Anthony went through the motions, not thinking much about pursuing a similar job after graduation. But as his time at the firm came to an end, he had a conversation with one of the men in the office that would ultimately define his career.

"So, what are your plans after you finish school?" the man asked.

Not one to mince words, Anthony replied, "No clue."

"What are your thoughts about working here? Could you see yourself doing this job?"

"It's been a great learning experience and I like the people I've met as well as how fast-paced the environment is, but I'm not sure I'm cut out for sales."

"Let me ask you something," the man leaned in, "do you keep in contact with your high school friends?"

Upon hearing this question, Anthony's eyes lit up, "It's literally the only thing I'm good at!"

"If that's the case, there's a job here if you want it when you graduate."

"What?" Anthony asked. "Why's that? I barely know anything about this job."

"The day-to-day skills can be learned. But the entirety of the job depends on advancing and developing long-term relationships. If you truly enjoy people and take pride in collecting friends, I think you'd do well here."

Fast-forward twenty years and working at this same financial institution is the only job Anthony's ever had. As the years passed and the relationships he built strengthened, he moved up the ranks and now the team he manages oversees over a billion dollars for families around the United States. More importantly, he's also been consistently the happiest person in my life. What's the reason for such professional and personal success?

Despite being the guy who stands near a keg at parties to have an excuse to talk to people instead of having to approach them, in Anthony's words, "I want people to win. I think they can feel that upon meeting me, and my follow-up actions demonstrate I want to do the best I can for them."

FRIENDSHIPS ARE A CHOICE

Growing up, although making friends with other kids may not have always been easy, being in school made the daunting task a little easier. If you attended a university, you probably experienced something similar. The bigger challenge for many of us, however, may have been finding time alone due to community living conditions.

Upon graduation, however, and depending on where you begin your career, forging close friendships can often become a struggle. As our adult responsibilities stack, a time comes when many of us look around and internally remark, "I swear I used to have friends. Where did everybody go?"

If you've experienced this struggle, you're not alone. In his book, *Social: Why Our Brains Are Wired to Connect*, author Matthew D. Lieberman presents a stark comparison between two surveys conducted almost twenty years apart. In the first survey conducted in 1985, the average response to the question of how many people participants had in their lives to discuss important matters was three. However, in the second survey conducted in 2004, the most common answer was zero. Shockingly, only 37 percent of respondents had three or more friends, a significant decrease from just two decades earlier.[1] This troubling trend has only continued since, as loneliness rates have more than doubled since the 1980s. Surgeon General of the United States Vivek

Murthy has even referred to the loneliness many of us are experiencing as an epidemic.[2]

If you're anything like me, you'll find these numbers terrifying. It's no secret that relationships and community involvement not only lead to increased happiness levels but also improved mental and physical health. And yet, despite living in a constantly connected world, most of us feel as if we are wandering through the day feeling what Sherry Turkle, professor of social sciences at MIT, so eloquently described as *alone together*.[3]

In the previous chapter, I stated that the reason I reached out to people was because I was curious to learn how to do what they were doing. That was only part of the story. A key motivator was that—at age thirty-eight—I felt lonely too.

At the time, my wife and I had moved to a small town an hour outside of Barcelona to be closer to her family. While we had each other and our two little boys, the realization that Spain would be my home for the foreseeable future had begun to hit me hard. I felt like I didn't have my own social group. Most days I was on kid duty while working to become 100 percent remote, while my wife continued to work in the city. I leaned into meeting the parents of my children's friends as well as my wife's friends. But I missed having my own group that was based on shared interest, rather than convenience. Meeting people passionate about writing about personal and professional development in English was hard to come by.

It was difficult to admit this to my wife. I didn't want her to feel like she and our boys weren't enough. Fortunately, I didn't have to explain much as she could feel that I was missing friendships of my own. So after moping around for a bit, and leaning on people like Anthony, I decided to do something about the loneliness I felt and pursued advancing the relationships I was building with other writers. I planned to turn our budding relationships into more than just online friends.

SLOW IS SMOOTH AND SMOOTH IS FAST

Being that one of my brothers, Greg, is a former Army Ranger and my dad served thirty years in the Air Force, I often heard the phrase growing up, "Slow is smooth and smooth is fast." In essence, this operating principle means the key to speed is making a commitment to take the right, small steps.

Following this creed, and taking things slow and specific with the people I reached out to ended up being a smart move. Even if they didn't reply in depth, their response quickly opened lines of communication. When they responded, rather than go for the ask, I'd advance the relationship by occasionally sending four types of messages:

- Short messages with things I thought they might find interesting like a book recommendation
- Ideas for an article by them I'd like to read
- A question they were the best suited to answer that wasn't easily found on Google
- Anything that said, "I saw this and thought of you."

It's important to note that I didn't do this with some grand strategy. I did it out of fear of rejection—which can sometimes be a beautiful thing. This may sound odd or even hard to believe if you're a millennial or younger, but many people in their forties and above, despite their title or background, feel like outsiders online as it's akin to learning a new language. Feeling like I wasn't good enough, however, forced me to ask: "What would it take to feel like I was good enough?" This simple question gave me the permission I was looking for to move at my own pace while taking note of different people's styles and engagement levels.

Much like how small talk is needed to make people feel comfortable offline so they have time to get a gauge on you, I learned the small touch points where I expressed curiosity inside and outside of their work, while revealing parts of myself when the circumstances allowed, which caused people to warm up to me. This taught me just how effective the "Rule of 8" can be as I discussed in the previous chapter. After all, who would you rather get to know? Someone who sends a one-off message before asking for your time? Or someone who shows consistent effort and interest while clearly wanting to get to know you as a person, and not because of what you can offer them?

By prioritizing my comfort zone online while taking into consideration other people's comfort levels, I no longer had to consider some clever introduction or give a ton of background on who I was when initially building these relationships. In each message requesting a call, I'd mention how much I appreciated their thoughts before asking if they'd be up to chat one day when they're out for a walk. Naturally, some people didn't reply or said no. This stung at times and made me question what I was doing. But then I'd remind myself of four fundamental truths:

- People have their own priorities
- Timing matters
- I wasn't made to connect with everyone
- Not everyone enjoys phone calls with people they don't know

Because I was asking people around my level—or they were a step above or below—a significant percentage said yes, which more than offset the occasional no.

MOVING FROM CONTACT TO CONNECTION

I'll never forget my first call with a "stranger." It was with Christopher Connors, keynote speaker and the author of the best-selling book, *Emotional Intelligence for the Modern Leader*. At the time, Christopher was working in corporate, and similar to me, he was trying to figure out his next move. When I suggested a call, he not only said yes but told me he admired how I was putting myself out there and one of his goals was to do the same.

The fact that Christopher lives in Charleston, South Carolina, helped to move along our first call as I'd spent a year living there in my late twenties. That commonality, our love of writing, and talking about the importance of taking the leap to meet new people, led to the call being over before I knew it. We made a pact to stay in touch after the call, and to this day, despite having five kids between us, we've done just that through quick, consistent follow-ups and phone calls.

But all the calls didn't go as well as the ones I had with Christopher. Some people and I just didn't click or the conversation didn't flow smoothly. Something interesting popped out in a handful of calls, though, so we'd keep in touch or support each other's work. After one particular conversation I thought didn't go well, I received a surprise message the following day saying how much they enjoyed talking. Then they said, "Working from home isn't all it's cracked up to be. I often feel like I'm working in a cave and you've inspired me to adopt your weekly habit."

This was a real eye-opening statement. By speaking to people each week across the globe, I realized that, yes, expanding their network was a driver that motivated many of them to get on a call. But of equal value, so was the fact that many of them simply craved human connection in a new world of remote and hybrid work where friendships aren't always easy to foster. When we put ourselves out there and take brave steps like connecting with people we find interesting, our days become more enjoyable and meaningful.

To hone this skill, however, takes intentionality. If you aim to effectively practice it, you have to make it a priority and you have to put in the effort. There are a lot of suggestions available to create and maintain friendships. The following proven suggestions from my experience and that of my network apply online as they do offline. I'm a big believer that online friends should never replace in-person friends because as human beings we physically need people in our lives. But when using technology for connection, it can be a heck of a tool to advance your relationships into ones that lead to real-world relationships. This begins with putting your own agenda aside and reserving time to keep track of the agenda of others.

THE ULTIMATE FRIENDSHIP CHEAT SHEET

Anthony, the man referenced at the onset of this chapter, learned early on in his career the lesson that no detail is too small. At any given time, he has 150–200 clients to keep up-to-date with who each wants—and expects—to feel like they are his only client. When I asked for his secret, he replied, "I have a terrible memory, so I cheat by being an avid note-taker. Remembering little things makes big things possible." Outside of work, Anthony does the same with his friends: he notes what they're up to along with setting calendar reminders of times to check in with them. But these notes aren't just general updates; they're specific things people have going on in their lives, like how their kid's little league game went or if a loved one is feeling any better after experiencing a health issue. He's known to also have soup delivered to both clients and friends if they aren't feeling well.

Throughout my experience in sales, my manager encouraged us to take a similar approach. During the first months of the job, he constantly hounded me after I finished a call. "Is the guy married?" he'd ask me, speaking a mile a minute. "If yes, what's his wife's name? What about kids? Does he have kids? Tell me you heard a dog barking in the background! I love dogs! What's his dog's name? Come on, Mike, you gotta know this stuff!"

Out of all the decisions I've made in my career, following Anthony and my manager's lead of carrying a notebook with me everywhere I go may very well be the most impactful. The key to maximizing the utility of this habit, however, is not just to track

86

our thoughts and list of to-dos but to also fill it up by keeping organized notes of what's important to other people and what they have going on in their lives.

Thanks to technology, within a couple of seconds we can check in on how things are going via text, email, or social media platforms. Think about it. How would you feel if prior to an interview you received a message saying, "They'd be lucky to have you." Pretty good, right? Or a message that read, "No need to reply as I know you have a lot going on, but I wanted to let you know I hope your mom is doing okay." Or even something as basic as a phone call on their birthday instead of a text or comment on Facebook. The times I recruit my kids to sing "Happy Birthday" alongside me are generally well received.

Maybe the notion of keeping track of what everyone in your orbit is up to sounds like a lot. The key is to not make it involve a lot of people. Although we may have one thousand friends on Instagram or LinkedIn, the odds are high that you'd like to better prioritize between half a dozen and two dozen people who you feel a deeper connection with. Hold these people tight. Make the effort. I've experienced the power of this practice firsthand. Most recently, multiple friends and writers reached out when my family went through a health crisis and their thoughtful message made a world of difference. When it comes to relationships, there's no such thing as "little acts of kindness." There's just kindness.

The important thing is not to keep score of who's doing what to support you. We all have our own challenges going on and if someone isn't checking in, check in with them. If I've learned anything about maintaining friendships, it's that sometimes it's up to us to take all ten steps to meet someone halfway.

FREQUENCY TRUMPS DURATION

According to a study shared by the *New York Times*, friendships that last are forged by making contact once every fifteen days.[4] This is a great thing to keep in mind. But it doesn't have to involve making a monumental effort or blocking hours on your calendar to tend to these relationships. Send them a funny video they may enjoy directly via text or email instead of posting it on social media for the world to see. Or maybe, if it's a childhood friend, share a recent photo and tell them you miss hanging out. Although physical connection can be a temporary fix, the true pain of loneliness often stems from the belief that we have no one to rely on, or no one to support. The innate desire to feel cared for and provide care is hardwired into the human condition, making loneliness an all-encompassing and deeply personal struggle.

Gretchen Rubin, author of *The Happiness Project*, shared on her podcast *Happier* that during quarantine she and a few friends sent a boring email each week sharing a few mundane life updates or experiences they had.[5] Starting a "weekly boring email chain" may sound odd, but the rationale for doing so is genius. The idea was sparked when Gretchen's mother made an insightful comment regarding our struggle to have fluid conversations as quarantine restrictions began to lift. "When you're in touch with a person all the time, you have a lot to say to each other, but when you see a person rarely, you have a hard time coming up with things to say," she states.

The power of this quirky exercise isn't necessarily about the information being shared; it's more about how effective sharing frequent daily life updates can be as they serve as jump-off points in conversations to get things moving. For example, if you bump into an old friend or when catching up on a call, it can be a struggle to get the conversation off the ground. So much has happened since the last time you talked that it's hard to know where to pick up. You probably aren't going to bring up the dynamite salad you made the other day or the fact that you finally beat your kid in Uno. So you fall into a slow dance of "What's up with you?" "Not much. What's up with you?"

The best part about Gretchen's recommendation is you don't even have to reply to the messages from the other members. You just have to read them so when you do talk, you can dive into your friend's newfound cooking skills or tactics to finally win at cards as it helps to grease the wheels for deeper conversations.

Like a lot of people in Spain, most of my friends here aren't interested in American-style self-help and business articles as they come off as guru-ish. Rather than fighting them on this, I made the habit of sending them a few articles each month, including my own, for them to let their frustrations out. This may sound weird, but it's been super effective in giving us something to talk about besides our kids when grabbing a drink. Once a week, I also take a long walk and leave voice messages for my buddies from home if they aren't able to hop on a call. Some people may not like voice messages. But I do and I share them with my friends who do also.

We're going to dig into how to do this at scale in the chapter, Make Room for Weak Ties. But figure out just one way to consistently follow up with the people you want in your life that works for you.

THE POWER OF GIVING AWAY YOUR BEST IDEAS FOR FREE

While writing this book, I linked up with Christopher Connors, the author of *Emotional Intelligence for the Modern Leader* who I mentioned earlier to discuss our first conversation. He told me what immediately stood out was how many ideas for his work I passed on to him, demonstrating I put a lot of thought into trying to create a connection with him. He reminded me that I encouraged him to lean into the lane of emotional intelligence for leaders as he clearly knew his stuff and I enjoyed his take. "I'll never forget that," he told me. "I don't know if my career would be where it is today without you planting that seed."

If you have an idea for someone, never hold it in. It's amazing how effective passing along messages like these can be: "I came across something that reminded me of you. I've really gotten a lot out of our conversations and I'm just throwing these ideas out there."

I told Christopher I liked his work in a specific lane and encouraged him to dig deeper into it. No matter your sector, there are ideas to be shared. One of my students from a recent course, Alex Grigoryev, who has a decade of experience in design-thinking and building course curriculums, offered to recreate an upcoming course with me to maximize its impact. The offer meant a lot. Today, as our relationship is expanding, we're also helping each other with our writing.

The entire purpose of collecting knowledge and experience is to pass it on to other people. Reserve time to think about what other people are hoping to achieve and consider how your skill set can amplify that. The habit of giving your best ideas away for free forces you to think beyond yourself, which is the core ingredient in building relationships that last. Much like an authentic compliment, you never know where one idea you have in passing may take someone. Plus, the odds are high that you're not going to have time to execute all the ideas that pop into your head anyway, so you might as well give them to other people to see what they do with them. Playing a role in someone making something cool is the definition of cool.

RISE UP BY BEING A "NAME-DROPPER"

When most people think of the term "name-dropper," they think of someone bragging incessantly about the big-name influencers they know. Sure, that's part of it, and it's not a great look. However, there's another kind of name-dropping the world could use more of: bragging about your friends to other people.

Consider how you'd feel if you learned a friend was talking you up to someone else. You'd feel amazing, right? Despite our uniqueness as human beings, we have more similarities than differences. A leading example is that we love it when other people speak highly of us. Not only that, but according to the phenomenon, spontaneous trait inferences or STI, how we talk about other people influences how those very people view us. Put simply, if you speak poorly of someone, people will associate the traits you used to describe the person with you also. Fortunately, STI swings both ways. If you want people to think highly of you, speak highly of other people.

The beauty of making an effort to get to know one person is that if you hit it off, you gain access to their network and vice versa. Whenever I meet someone new, I try my best to connect them to someone with similar interests or someone who has a skill set that could help advance their own skills. Today, a handful of these people have formed thriving businesses together. Playing a small part in that has helped us grow closer as the foundation of the relationship is rooted in mutual giving.

Name-drop the hell out of people you admire. Quietly build a reputation as a connector. Give out-on-a-limb recommendations to people you see potential in and those who didn't have the privilege of the same starting line as you. Out of all the connections I've helped facilitate, few have been more rewarding than getting up-and-comers who could use a lift in front of friends looking for some help. Of course, your reputation is attached to the recommendation. Networking doesn't have to involve frantically handing out other people's business cards like a crazed salesperson. If you've had a genuinely positive experience with someone or see incredible potential in them, consider casually mentioning their name in conversations and suggest that others get to know them. After all, our lives aren't solely defined by who inspires us, but rather by our willingness to help and support each other.

WHAT GETS PLANNED GETS PRIORITIZED

When navigating my career change, I expressed anxiety over the gnawing feeling that I was prioritizing work over friendships and especially my wife and kids. I felt like a fraud being someone who works in the social facilitation field. My mindfulness coach and now close friend Justin Caffrey recommended something so simple it's genius: "Get your nonnegotiable family and friend times on your schedule first before filling it with work stuff prior to every Sunday night."

The key to Anthony's ability to keep both his clients and friendships front and center follows a similar thread as Justin's. Anthony recommends "automating as much as you can." He breaks out his calendar to get the next meetup or call on the books before their time together is over. Creating "standing" or "recurring" meetups either weekly, monthly, quarterly, or even yearly is also an effective tool in ensuring the people you want in your life remain a fixture in your life. This could entail organizing a monthly hike on the last Saturday of each month with a group of people you'd like to see more. Or if it's for friends who no longer live close to you, putting together a bimonthly video call. Every Thursday, my friend Joan in Spain hosts a weekly dinner. As for Anthony, he organizes a weekend getaway every spring for our high school buddies in addition to his regularly scheduled interactions.

Make a list of the people in your life. Who are your weekly, monthly, quarterly, or even yearly friends? This may sound harsh, like we're labeling people or putting them in buckets. The reality is we only have so much time and the people who matter most should be prioritized. For Anthony, he wants to be in touch with his best friends every week, while also meeting up with them or having a call at least once a month. For his second-layer friends, he wants to be in touch every month, while planning to meet up a few times a year.

The thing that stands out about Anthony and all of the people I know who have strong relationships is they genuinely like people and take great pride in being there for them. "Being the type of person people can trust to be there for them through the bad times is crucial," he told me. "But nothing lights me up more than learning I'm one of the first people someone calls when they're winning and I take a lot of pride in being someone they want to celebrate with."

This will take effort, but as Kevin Kelley eloquently told me, "The best things in life demand *effortfulness*. A handmade gift for your spouse trumps an expensive one you bought on Amazon. Making the effort to call or ideally see someone face to face—either for business or pleasure—will always lead to tighter bonds than digital." Kevin's right. After all, when was the last time you heard someone say their favorite memories take place on Facebook?

Prioritizing weekly calls with new people and reserving time to advance and maintain my existing relationships bring not only fulfillment but also a lot of ideas. My career is nothing but having interesting conversations and taking the time to distill what I'm learning so more people can benefit from the thoughtful, good people in my life.

But you don't need to go over the top and try to be everything to a million people. In fact, the gold lies where you make a commitment to go small while making room for weak ties.

Small Is the New Big

I REMEMBER THE EXACT MOMENT MY WRITING AND COACHING career went on the offensive. It was 8:31 on the morning of Saturday, February 9, 2019. I'd spent the night sleeping on the floor next to my one-year-old son Luc's crib. I woke up to find him staring at me through his bed bars with a massive smile on his face, completely oblivious to the torture he'd put me through the night before. As I stood up to stretch and cast a familiar look of both love and loathing that most parents can relate to, I grabbed my phone to check the time and I immediately noticed a flood of notifications.

"This can't be right," I thought to myself, "thirty-seven new messages?"

In between trying to persuade Luc to go to sleep and waking up with a crooked back in a small mountain town in Spain, I discovered that a big-name blogger six thousand miles away in New York City had liked the article so much that she linked it to her newsletter.

"Laia!" I screamed. I didn't care how early it was or that my wife was asleep. "You're not going to believe it! I think I actually did something good!" Her response? A similar look of both love and loathing that I gave Luc for waking her up that most married couples can also relate to.

But I didn't let her response deter me from hosting a party of one to celebrate the good news. For the next forty-eight hours, I was an absent father and husband. Like a bee on a honey biscuit, my eyes remained glued to my phone as the views and messages skyrocketed.

100,000 views.

150,000 views.

200,000 views.

Thanks to the magic touch of Joanna Goddard, the founder of the mega-popular blog *Cup of Jo*, the article hit well over a quarter of a million views. *The best part?* It was an article about the lessons I'd learned on what it takes to lead a life where I wake up smiling most mornings. No slick marketing message needed. No pushing services. No commanding voice of "You need to do this to succeed!"

In fact, within the article, I talked about many of the dumb decisions I'd made in life and the shifts I'd made to rectify them. The positive response to my honest story took me off guard. Equally shocking was the number of people asking to work with me snce I thought talking about struggling with anxiety would do more harm than good to my "personal brand."

But the reason the article went viral wasn't all me—far from it. Nor was it only because of Joanna Goddard's wizardry. The reason both the piece and my career took off is because, while I continued to make weekly calls, I'd taken the time to build a small community of people who had committed to help each other grow together.

ONE DECISION CAN CHANGE YOUR LIFE

When I started reaching out to people, a twenty-five-year-old German writer named Niklas Goeke was first on my list as he was my inspiration to start writing online. Nik's work reminded me of Seth Godin who is perhaps the most well-respected operator in the creator space with close to two dozen best-sellers under his belt. After watching a YouTube video of Nik dancing to techno in his bedroom just one day after reading one of the most thought-provoking articles I'd come across, I had to know how a shy kid from a small town in Germany found the courage so quickly to be no one other than himself.

Despite my eagerness to connect, I was hesitant to contact him. I thought he'd be too busy and my work wasn't where it needed to be yet. Fortunately, I didn't have to stress too much about our potential call because once I shot him a message to talk, his response was short: "No. I'm not doing any calls for the next three months to focus on a project." One hundred days later, while I continued with my weekly outreach and call habit, I reached out again. "Sounds good," he replied. "I appreciate your patience."

While Nik was working on his project and I continued my habit of reaching out to other writers, the seed of an idea kept growing in my head. It was fun getting to know different people as our shared love of writing made for good conversations. But there was only one problem: after a great first date, it became harder and harder to stay in touch with a growing list of people, some of whom I really hit it off with. Then one day it dawned on me, "Why not see if a few of the people I'm connecting with would be interested in starting a little mastermind group to get to know each other and support each other's work?"

Once Nik and I finally linked up, it was clear that the mutual respect of putting fears aside and going after what we wanted was there. When I explained the idea I had brewing about creating a mastermind group in Slack and asked him if he was up for joining, I knew that his buy-in would speed up the process. Again, however, his response was swift, "No. Not my thing." We wrapped things up and went our separate ways.

But something interesting happened a week later. Out of the blue, he sent me a message. "Screw it, I'm in. Working alone gets boring. I'm talking to a lot of the people you've mentioned about getting involved in some form or another anyway. Let's get this thing moving. What do you need me to do?"

I'll never forget that reply. I didn't have an online presence, but here was a guy with a six-figure audience saying he was down to team up. As a novice in organizing online groups and Slack, I went with my go-to approach: I asked for help.

Before officially opening the doors, a few members and I organized a handful of basic operating principles and norms to ensure engagement and respect from the start. In addition to each member committing to a minimum of a weekly check-in to bat around ideas, these included the following principles:

- Setting a clear initial group goal (which was helping each other improve our writing and grow on LinkedIn).

- Mandatory detailed introduction messages from all group members explaining our professional goals and random tidbits about who we are outside of work.

- Facilitating calls between members who shared common interests and who hadn't yet spoken with each other.

- Attending monthly group calls.

Thanks to taking these measures, once the doors opened, despite only a dozen initial members, the messages inside the space quickly escalated to over two thousand a week. To ensure the engagement stuck, I turned to many of the habits discussed in the previous chapter of keeping an "other people's to-do" list. I gave away a ton of ideas for free and "name-dropped" members with other writers I was meeting which often led to new connections being formed outside the group. Since many of the people involved weren't the outgoing types and got tired of endless self-promotion, we designed a way to promote each other's work through a hashtag we created for LinkedIn, #quoteyourconnections. This turned out to be smart on multiple fronts.

- First, status updates saying, "Enough with the Tony Robbins quotes, quote the good people in your life instead," stood out and resonated with people who were tired of big-name thought leaders.
- Second, it made social media actually social.
- Third, to generate content for each other to post, each member had to read some of the other members' work, helping us to gain a deeper understanding of each other's style, values, and story.

This last point—digging into each other's story—was crucial. As mentioned in Principle 4, learning about the challenges someone has overcome and the reasons behind their beliefs and actions can command respect. After six months, as a result of sharing feedback, exchanging resources, and collaborating on projects, the articles of many people in the group began to take off. The most poignant moment for me regarding my career occurred when my friend Nick Wignall (who I referenced in Principle 2, "Lead with Listening") helped improve an article by suggesting a more enticing title. Thanks to his feedback, and the support of others who regularly helped me improve my writing, the article ended up on the kitchen table of *Cup of Jo*, and propelled me from an unknown creator and coach to a slightly less unknown one today.

Similar to how organizations have advisory boards, the group served as a collective think tank to help each of us navigate our new world way of working. Being that we were scattered all over the globe, at different stages of our careers, and the group consisted of people ranging from twenty-two years old to forty-five years old, the insights we gleaned from each other allowed us to see our work through new angles which helped reveal our blind spots. The more we got to know each other and collaborated, the more our relationships extended past our work. We held in-person retreats to hang out and met up for long weekends when possible.

Taking the initiative to form this initial group was the best decision I've made in my career. Guy Raz, the host of multiple hit podcasts including *How I Built This*, once remarked, "Creativity comes from intense collaboration." This speaks directly to my experience forming this group. Working with a dozen other creators who each brought a different lens to the table solidified my belief that the difference between good and great is other people's input. Together, by carving out our own little corner and working collaboratively to grow, we created the individualized noise we wanted to hear in the world. Of equal importance, it made work more fun. The group provided a welcome break from our day jobs or the isolation that many self-employed people experience when working in solitude.

The experience didn't come without its mistakes. Rather than listening to my gut to keep it small, after the second year, I opened the doors to other writers I was speaking with on my weekly calls as well as recommendations from other members. A year later, rather than just a dozen people, the group grew to fifty members. Like most things that grow too fast while being led by a novice online community builder, the engagement dropped. The effort to keep that many people invested wasn't something I wanted to do or enjoyed doing.

This mistake had its benefits however. Being exposed to such a large number of creators day in and day out—while also doing quick collaborations with many of them—gave me a front-row seat to their goals, values, communication style, strengths, and work process. As time passed, it became clear that the connection I had with a dozen people was stronger than that of other members and we had established a proven track record of working well together.

Deciding to leave the big group in favor of joining small groups was difficult, given that forming the group had given me so much. Yet, the experience reinforced the notion that I thrive when digging deep with a select few rather than leading larger groups or teams.

You Don't Need a Big Network—You Need a Supportive One

Robin Dunbar, a British anthropologist, gained fame in the early 1990s when he published a research study that demonstrated human beings aren't designed to maintain more than 150 meaningful relationships, ultimately earning the moniker "Dunbar's number."[1]

Throughout history, Dunbar's findings show that groups often splinter once they extend past 150 members to ensure bonds and engagement stay tight. If you look at military units throughout history, and even growing startups and established organizations today, similar numbers shine through as either new departments or offices are often opened once groups approach the 150-person marker.

More recently, some researchers have set out to debunk Dunbar's number. A leading proponent, Johan Lind, associate professor and researcher at Stockholm University in Sweden, argues the number of relationships human beings can have is limitless. In a *New York Times* article from 2021, "Can You Have More Than 150 Friends?," Lind is quoted as saying, "We can learn thousands of digits of pi, and if we engage with lots of people, then we will become better at having relationships with lots of people."[2]

It's hard to argue with some of Dunbar's proponents that the world has changed since his study was released three decades ago. Due to technology, we now socialize and work in radically different ways. Social media and other networking and communication tools help make managing large numbers of connections easier.

Whether Dunbar is right or Lind is right, however, is irrelevant. Human beings are complex. We each thrive in different ways. What works for me may not work for you. It's up to each of us to identify the size of the network that's best for us as individuals.

The problem is that we're trained to believe that "bigger is better" and the signpost of success is "more." This could be either money, follower count, or the size of our network. But more doesn't always mean better; sometimes more just means more.

From my perspective, Dunbar and his proponents are arguing in the wrong direction. I'd state that having and trying to keep up with 150 *friends* is nuts. It's as if the definition of "friendship" has lost its meaning since the advent of Facebook. Sure, today we have the option to have way more than 150 contacts or acquaintants. But are all of these people actually friends? Are we really spending enough time with each of them to the extent we know what's running through their heads and beating through their hearts?

Some people enjoy and receive their energy from having a large network. They like big group settings, look forward to going to large events, and weave with ease between different social groups. Others prefer more intimate gatherings and connections. This isn't a jab at the former and praise for the latter. I'm simply stating a fact that we all thrive in different ways and it's those differences that give the world color.

I know a lot of people due to the nature of my work as a teacher, consultant, and writer, as well as being someone who enjoys visiting new places and has lived on three different continents. I care about all of them as human beings. But I also know that a small percentage of them add the most value to my life. For me, our network isn't about maximizing the *quantity* of people we know, it's about optimizing the *quality* of connection and closeness we feel for people.

The big question we must ask is, how do you determine the difference between those who should be part of your *tight network* and those who you should keep as *weak ties*? What I mean by *weak ties* refers to those outside of our immediate circle who still contribute value to our personal and professional lives (we'll explore this concept more in the following chapter). Is there a way to make this complicated yet highly important decision easier?

THE POWER OF BUILDING A "PATCHWORK" NETWORK

During the first week of COVID-19 quarantine, after acknowledging how much the situation sucked, my wife, Laia, noted a clever way to identify who matters most to us. "One silver lining is that this experience has provided us with a clear understanding of the people we want to prioritize in our lives. Think about it. We can easily look at our phone to see who we first reached out to and rely on as well as who we drop whatever we're doing to support when they need us."

I thought this observation was really insightful. Regardless of the pandemic, it's a good exercise to do from time to time. Rather than a friendship audit of identifying the people who aren't adding value to your life as many people recommend doing, the beauty of my wife's exercise is it allows you to identify the right people and optimize them first on your calendar. By doing so, you won't need to spend much time thinking about who isn't adding value to your life as you're already filling it with those who do.

When doing my wife's exercise, one thing became abundantly clear: it didn't include 150 people. Outside of my family, which includes my two lifelong best friends Ian Rosario and Steven Gleich, my pandemic friendship list consisted of half a dozen of my closest friends, followed by my closest work collaboration partners. On top of being grateful for them, these are the people that I want to say my name when they think about the handful of individuals whom they're most grateful for. These relationships go past pleasure and convenience as they are rooted in mutual admiration, respect, and trust. They serve as the people who we don't hesitate to ask for help from each other and show up no matter the inconvenience. When the worlds of two people who not only enjoy each other's company but are there for one another through thick and thin collide, it serves as the initial spark for one plus one to someday equal three.

But outside of enjoying, trusting, and admiring this handful of people, what is it about them that allows us to comfortably excel together? Are enjoyment, trust, and admiration enough to make career waves? Or is there more to it? Is there something that goes past my group of work friends that can potentially apply to all of us?

Kevin Kelley, my writing partner whose bicoastal strategic design firm, Shook Kelley, has thrived for over three decades, shared an invaluable piece of advice. By identifying how our skill sets complement each other, we can scale the fun, trust, and admiration we have with certain workmates to enhance each other's work.

When he and his team look at potential new hires—in addition to identifying if they're a culture fit—they evaluate the candidates through the following lens:

- Are they starters (those who are good with filling a blank page)?
- Are they developers (those who are good with running with the initial seed of an idea)?
- Or, are they finishers (those who are good at applying the finishing touches and getting projects to shine)?

If you are self-aware of your skill set, surrounding yourself with people who have different skill sets allows you to build a network where your shortcomings are covered by your partners' strengths. Ultimately, this creates a "patchwork" network where the best bits of different people create something stronger than what you could have done on your own.

I get excited when I have a new idea. But being a starter is not my true strength and neither is combing through the final details to tie up loose ends. I shine, however, as a developer. I love nothing more than digging in with someone or a small team of people to advance initial ideas and untangle all the knots before passing it off to someone who excels at patching together the finishing touches to take an idea that's an eight to make it a ten.

For example, both Kevin and Kim Dabbs, the author of *You Belong Here* and a collaboration partner I've worked with a great deal since the pandemic, are tremendous starters. They can get a page filled out in an hour, whereas the same idea may take me a week to get moving. On the opposite end of a project, my friend Stephen Moore is a heck of a tightener. He loves his role of getting ideas ready to introduce to the world. I work well with each of these people because our relationship is based on progress. By having complementary skill sets and focusing on our individual strengths, we not only save time by working together, but it also makes work more enjoyable as our relationship is rooted in taking a good idea and collaborating to make it great.

When working with my students in their master's project management course, whenever Kevin brings up this exercise during a guest lecture their eyes widen as they scramble to take notes. Twice, I've heard a student in different classes say, "Holy shit!" as the lightbulb regarding Kevin's suggestion exploded in their heads. They immediately think about who in their network they are best positioned to work with to help move each other's ideas from zero to ten.

The beauty of identifying people with contrasting skill sets— that complement each other's skill set—is that the relationship is rooted in getting things right, rather than arguing about who's right. This is because the shared goal of working together to make a valuable contribution to the world comes first, second, and third. These are the relationships where you can yell at each other like banshees one minute about the best way to take something and laugh the next about a quirky thing that happened during the discussion. If you were to eavesdrop on a conversation with any of the collaboration partners I have, you'd be hard-pressed to identify whether we are best friends or mortal enemies due to the equal mix of laughter and arguing. These are the people you can *happily fight with* as the shared goal isn't individual advancement but rather collective progress.

GO BIG BY CARING FOR YOUR SMALL

When looking to build out your network, think about your own strengths and weaknesses as well as those of your colleagues to identify collaboration partners that you not only like and trust but also enlarge your own work and vice versa. Seek out these relationships. It's not a coincidence that as a business grows, founding teams create a board of advisors and bring on teammates who cover areas that aren't their strong suit to not only move faster but create better products and deliver higher-quality services.

No one is stopping us from doing the same thing.

No matter if we're self-employed or working for a company, we're all responsible for treating our careers like our own businesses to successfully navigate the winds of never-ending change in today's uncertain landscape. That doesn't mean, however, that we should treat our careers as a one-person business.

If starting a group to collectively make some noise isn't your thing, or you don't yet have a tight group of people who hold different strengths to help each other, consider joining one of the many big groups available today on platforms like Slack and Discord. It's a good way to quickly meet people who hold varying skill sets while observing how they operate and picking up on what their values are as well as getting an idea of how well you could potentially work together. Few things will help you identify your long-term collaboration partners faster than proactively putting yourself in a position where you can quickly collaborate with a lot of people. The chances are good you'll connect with at least one person during the process, which opens the door to supporting each other in a more intimate setting. It may take some time. Don't get discouraged. It took me working day in and day out with four dozen creatives for a year before the signals strengthened. But I wouldn't have wanted it any other way. It allowed us to see how well we got along, how well our values aligned, whether or not we had similar missions, and how well we worked together beyond the initial attraction.

When you find these people, hold them tight. Go to the end of the world for them. Keep tabs on what's important to them both inside and outside of their work. Ask yourself what you can do with what you have to make their lives better and their career bigger.

As a way to thank Nik Goeke for his invaluable help, I reached out to famed author Seth Godin, who is one of Nik's favorite creators, to request a favor. In my message to Seth, I highlighted Nik's persistent generosity toward countless people, which I knew was a core value for Seth, and included one of Nik's best articles. I then asked Seth if he would be willing to send a quick message of encouragement to Nik. Less than ten minutes later, Seth replied, and the next day, Nik called me to say, "You won't believe what just happened! Seth Godin just told me I have talent and to keep at it!"

My mom once told me that the key to both changing the world and happiness is to keep your world small and to care deeply about the people you're fortunate to walk and work through life with. We all want to do meaningful work and few things will expedite this process faster than seeking out the people who mean a great deal to you. It's hard to say if Nik and I will continue to support each other years into the future. But as we continue to show up for each other through both the good and bad of life, my gut says we will. This is because the more struggles you go through with someone, the tighter friendships become.

Just don't get so comfortable that you stop making the effort to learn how the other half lives. Diversity in relationships is a core ingredient to leading a rich life. To gain access to different ideas and perspectives, make the effort to build and maintain "weak ties."

PRINCIPLE 8

Gain New Eyes through the Power of Weak Ties

ONE OF THE MOST IMPACTFUL CONVERSATIONS OF MY LIFE TOOK place with my dad. I had to travel from Barcelona to San Jose, Costa Rica, for work. Being that he lives in the United States and my mom had plans with her friends, he took the opportunity to meet me as it'd been a few years since we'd last seen each other.

At the time, my wife and I recently had our first child. I was attempting to juggle living in a different country while finding work that lit me up, and most poignantly, navigating the big life change of becoming a father. Inevitably, given my circumstances, our conversations veered heavily toward parenting and, ultimately, how to make the most out of life as our responsibilities grow. My dad said some really smart things during our time together. This is particularly true when he talked about the realities of aging as he said something that hit me equally hard in both my head and heart—"The saddest part about getting older for me is seeing how intellectually dead some of my friends have chosen to become."

Although it's been nearly a decade since he said these words, I've yet to come across a more impactful warning regarding how to waste your life. He went on to tell me that it was as if the day Cal Ripken retired from baseball, some of his friends had chosen to retire from life. They barely leave their house. They rarely read a book. When they do talk to people, it's the same old friends they've had for eons who share similar worldviews. As a result, instead of chasing the day, both their bodies and minds have begun to wither away.

I'd been told a million times previously about the importance of being curious. But the way my dad carefully crafted his message through his use of the words "intellectually dead" and "choosing" made me internalize the message. At that moment, I realized life isn't about being the smartest person in the room. Nor is it about being the fastest, the strongest, or making enough money to fly to the moon. Life is about being persistently curious; it's about learning something new, seeing somewhere new, and meeting someone new. As my dad implied, life's about choosing to be *intellectually alive*.

But being intellectually alive isn't only about being open-minded when presented with new ideas and perspectives. It's about proactively seeking out these experiences. It's about fighting to break free of the bubble that's so easy to create for ourselves to understand how the other 99.9 percent of humanity lives outside of those who look, think, or act like us. By doing so, we gain access to not only new ways of looking at the world but also opportunities we may not have otherwise heard about. It's about creating space in our lives to reap the many benefits of "weak tie" relationships.

CREATE STRONG OPPORTUNITIES THROUGH THE POWER OF WEAK TIES

Our weak ties refer to the relationships we have with acquaintances or colleagues who aren't part of our inner circle or who we do not closely work with. The usage of the word "weak," however, is a bit misleading. The term was introduced in 1973 via a paper published by sociologist Mark Granovetter aptly titled, "The Strength of Weak Ties" in the *American Journal of Sociology*.[1] The meat and potatoes of Granovetter's study argue that, yes, close friends and family are instrumental in emotional support. But in terms of being presented with new opportunities and learning new information, it's our "weak ties" that hold the most strength.

This may not make immediate logical sense, but the rationale does make sense. The chances are good that your closest friends share similar interests, have similar conversations, and run in similar circles which lead them to hear about the same kinds of opportunities and a subset of ideas. Those on the outside of your primary network, however, live a different experience. They have their own social group and are exposed to different opportunities and ways of thinking.

I've found Granovetter's findings to be dead on. Regarding opportunities, except for a managerial role that came with a salary, all of my positions in my twenty-year career have either been straight commission or some variation of self-employed. No matter what I was doing or the sector I was working in, I've been fortunate to have a few spokespeople blast my name around their network despite not spending a lot of time together or in many cases, ever meeting in person. These are the people I either met randomly through work, social events, mutual friends, or in some cases, through other weak ties.

For example, the opportunities I have today to help write books in the "Business for Good" space, are a direct result of one weak tie relationship. In 2020, I received a message from a talented connector named Anne Palmer to talk about possibly helping out with her writing. Life got in the way of the two of us working together. But shortly after we spoke, she connected me with Fred Dust, the author of *Making Conversation* and former Global Managing Director of IDEO. Anne did this without any ulterior motive other than thinking Fred and I could benefit from getting to know each other. Not thirty seconds into talking to Fred, I understood Anne's deep admiration for him. He is very much his own person and a heck of a storyteller. Like Anne, Fred is also the type of person who seems to know everyone. He's like the Kevin Bacon of the social impact and creative world. Due to his love of seeing people make cool stuff together, whenever anyone in his wide circle says they're interested in writing, it seems like he drops my name. This makes it very hard to refer to Fred as a weak tie as the strength of my career is a direct reflection of Fred's giving and generous spirit.

But I'm far from the only person who has benefited from weak ties regarding gaining exposure to opportunities. In September 2022, LinkedIn published a study that tracked twenty million users of the platform between 2015 and 2019.[2] The results reinforce the strength of weak ties and the importance of keeping up with casual acquaintances. Senior editor at large at Linkedin, George Anders, shared a few examples from the study in a LinkedIn article where people landed new jobs or were able to navigate changing sectors thanks to weak tie relationships.[3] In one case, a woman who ran a music-marketing consultancy, as well as a local music store, was forced to close the doors of both of her businesses because of the pandemic. A man who had taken music lessons in her store, however, caught wind that she was on the lookout for a job and he referred her to his fast-growing marketing firm. Despite being well-connected in the music industry, her direct network couldn't offer much help because they were in the same predicament due to the damage the pandemic caused to the industry. Ironically, it was the "weak tie" of a former student that proved the most beneficial to the woman's career as opposed to her inner circle. In another case, a middle school teacher was looking for a career change. The person who set off a chain of events that helped this former teacher transition into a new career path was a woman she was in the marching band with in high school. When I reflect on this study, as well as many of my friends who have benefited from weak ties, and my own experiences, it's hard not to view weak ties as a crucial element in creating "career luck."

While weak ties might provide us with opportunities we might not normally be exposed to from our close ties, perhaps the greatest benefit is that they provide us access to new ideas and ideologies that help us become more innovative.

Escape the Echo Chamber

As human beings, we have a natural inclination to stay within our comfort zone, seeking out and surrounding ourselves with people who share similar perspectives, beliefs, and lifestyles. While there is nothing inherently wrong with doing so, we put ourselves at risk of closing ourselves off from the outside world and missing out on learning opportunities and ideas from those who've lived a different experience. Our critical thinking skills decline when we only surround ourselves with people who think, look, and act like us, leading us to succumb to groupthink and limiting our ability to challenge and grow our beliefs. This mindset is more commonly known as an "echo chamber" in pop culture where we only see, hear, and agree with the content and ideologies we'd be inclined to support.

The online world we live in and the associated algorithms make it even harder to break free of this cycle. We click on an article, video, or website, and the next day our "curated" feeds literally dish out more of the same. As this information stacks, the more we begin to think the world is like us instead of seeing diversity of thought and experiences for the gift that it is.

A recent article by the Brookings Institution concluded that YouTube's recommendation algorithm has the potential to reinforce ideological biases that lead users down "rabbit holes" of extremist content. The authors conducted a study analyzing YouTube's recommended videos for political and social issue-related searches and found that the algorithm frequently recommended videos with extreme views, often leading to more extreme content. Additionally, the study found that users who watched these recommended videos were more likely to have their beliefs reinforced rather than challenged.[4]

For creativity and innovation to thrive, however, we need different outlooks and perspectives to challenge us. If every day we have the same conversations with the same people that reinforce what we already believe to be true, it's only a matter of time before we view anyone else who doesn't hold that belief as against us. Of course, we can read books to learn new concepts, listen to podcasts outside our day-to-day normal listening, and make friends with ChatGPT. But this learning loses serious points if it's not being discussed in a considerate and open-minded way with others who see the world differently than we do. We miss out on the power of personal stories that uncover why people believe what they believe and why it is they do what they do. When we understand someone's reasons for their actions and the thought process behind their decisions, we may still not share the same views, but we see their humanity which can lead to a greater level of respect.

The importance of weak ties lies in gaining access to new perspectives and creating what some refer to as "idea sex," where two people's ideas combine to create a third. For me, learning about other people's experiences and perspectives is the leading benefit. We may not see diversity of conversation as part of the creative process or career advancement. But to have new ideas, we need to expose ourselves to different inputs. This makes proactively seeking out relationships with diverse perspectives or those who hold opposing beliefs to learn their point of view critical as our eyes open to how other people see and experience the world. Doing so is the antidote to becoming intellectually dead, and it is also how we can continue to strengthen our understanding and empathy.

I'm not a fan of speaking in absolutes and I'm hesitant to say the world would be a better place if we all did one thing. But I think the world would be a better place if we didn't shy away from contacting people who hold different views or challenge our opinions. Reaching out to someone and saying, "I'd never thought of that from that angle. I'd love to talk with you about this as your take opened my eyes to a perspective I hadn't considered," not only lowers fences but has the potential to punch through ceilings as change tends to happen when both sides of the issue work with each other.

As stated, this doesn't mean we have to run over to their side. We weigh perspectives to understand how the other half lives, which adds weight to our own arguments. It seems as though we can't be friends with people who hold different views today. It's up to each of us to end this absurdity and the only way I know how to do this is through getting to know other humans and being open to how they came to believe what they believe. Prioritizing making room for weak ties across an array of ages, backgrounds, and locations only reinforces the fact that more than one truth can exist in the world.

When One Plus One Equals Three

Because very few ideas today are truly original, once we escape our echo chambers and allow other people's perspectives to inform our creativity, we create something new. Maintaining weak ties has two obvious benefits. First, it helps us gain new perspectives and understand different viewpoints, which can add weight to our own truth as we're doing the work of pressure-testing them. Second, it allows us to break out of our day-to-day routines and make new connections between ideas. By seeking out different experiences and insights, we can add depth and color to our ideas. The combination of sharing our experiences and what we learn from people who have different views is the fastest way for one plus one to equal three.

When I began the habit of reaching out to one new person a week, I stuck mainly with other writers operating in the personal and professional development space, and I am glad I started there. Connecting with people who share similar interests makes it easier to take the uncomfortable step of reaching out to strangers. Throughout this process, discovering the thought processes of someone who was approaching a similar topic from another angle exposed me to a new way of looking at something, which made my work better. Asking people what they think about something you're working on and receiving comments that begin with sage advice like, "Have you thought about this . . . ?" is often the spark that moves good ideas to great ones.

Over the years, my calls have expanded to include anyone doing something I think is interesting or I view as impactful. This ranges from people working at nonprofits and leaders at for-profit organizations to seventeen-year-olds and seventy-one-year-olds across the globe in an array of sectors as well as artists across a wide range of mediums. Being that I live outside my home country—and due to the nature of my work as a teacher with students from all over the world—most days I'm exposed to ideas I hadn't considered before. This has not only played a significant role in my writing and consulting career as I'm able to pull ideas from different people together, but I'm also way less judgmental than I used to be. Rather than thinking my way of viewing or doing something is the only way, by getting to know people with a different lived experience, I've learned firsthand that no matter someone's title or background, there is something to be learned from them.

Today, I couldn't imagine not proactively seeking out these conversations. The world is changing at warp speed. Speaking to people younger than I am in different corners of the globe offers a glimpse into how they are navigating the new world we live in. On the other end of the spectrum, those who are older are a gold mine for learning what's worth keeping from the old world and what matters most in life. The LinkedIn weak ties study mentioned previously backs this: "The weak-ties concept is based on the idea that you'll see a wider range of possibilities if you tap into people who attended different schools, who might be noticeably older or younger than you, and whose exact career journeys don't mirror yours." In short, diversity gives both the world and our careers color.

It's easy to think that when we're working in a sector we should connect with people in that sector. When we go on places like X, it's hard not to buy into the narrative that growth comes from seeking out relationships with people ahead of us in the area we are working in. Hell, the algorithm keeps us engaged by feeding our preexisting interests and seems to reward people for staying in their lane. But you have to ask yourself: is this really making my work better? Or would I be better off getting to know and maintain relationships with people who are pursuing other interests?

For instance, if you're a graphic designer networking with startup founders, small business owners across an array of sectors, writers, or podcast hosts can open up more opportunities than solely connecting with other graphic designers. This is because graphic designers rarely hire other graphic designers. The same is true for idea generation—seeking out fresh perspectives from outside the graphic design community can lead to the creation of new trends, rather than simply following existing ones.

Of course, managing weak ties can be a challenge, especially if you have a lot of them. I'd never see my wife and kids if I followed up regularly with each of my weak ties. But that's where the beauty of technology and creating a system that works for you comes into play. Doing so makes it easy to stay top of mind with people outside of our primary network and continue to reap the benefits of weak ties without sacrificing valuable time with our loved ones.

KEEP YOUR WEAK TIES STRONG

While writing this book, I reached out to George Anders, the senior editor at large at LinkedIn, who I referenced earlier in the chapter regarding the study on weak ties. I asked George if he had any actionable advice to keep weak ties strong to reap the benefits from them throughout our careers. He shared a great tip that is equally as impactful as it is time-effective.

"I've found that there is good cheer and good value in sending people a warm and personalized congratulations note when they get a new job. Especially if I have absolutely nothing to ask from them at the time," George told me. "Being able to reference some shared moment that we had a while ago or something light-hearted about their line of work helps make it authentic rather than just mechanical. An example of this light-hearted message would look something like, 'It's hard to believe that just three years ago, we were trying to scrounge a free dinner out of the bar snacks at the Ramada in Chicago.'" George concluded his wisdom by saying that when we make the effort to do things like this people are more likely to respond if six months later we have a more substantial request.

I thought his advice was really smart. On platforms like LinkedIn, we get notifications when someone in our network is starting a new job and many people share the projects they are excited about starting. Taking a moment to leave a personalized message is memorable. It stands out among a sea of either no congratulations or auto-responses platforms often suggest. Taking the extra one-minute effort a few times during the month as your contacts venture into new opportunities may be all you need to keep these weak ties strong.

Similar to George, rather than waiting until I potentially need something from one of my weak ties, I have my way of keeping them warm that is authentic to my way of doing things. This entails sending a minimum of two of the five types of quick messages each week.

They are as follows:

- **A "Thank-You" message:** As stated in Principle 5, "Get to Know Your Heroes," people love to feel appreciated. This could come in the form of reaching out to someone you studied with thanking them for helping you pass an exam or a past coworker who jumped in to lend a hand when you needed it. This simple act keeps lines of communication open.

- **A message to someone you know doing admirable work:** Reaching out to people you admire that you don't yet know is a good habit to form. But don't forget about the people you already know who are doing valuable work. If someone just changed sectors and is venturing into a new career path, let them know how brave you think they are. If you ever feel the pull to change course, sending this type of message opens the door to following up with them when you have questions.

- **A message to someone you recently met:** Maybe this new connection came from a mutual friend or someone you crossed paths with at an event. Sharing why you specifically enjoyed speaking with them is often all it takes to warm up this weak tie.

- **A message to a friend with whom you fell out of contact:** The easiest way to have friends is to keep up with old ones. Sending a quick, "I thought of you today when [insert memory spark]," is often received well. Many of my high school and college friends are doing wildly different things today than they did two decades ago when we began our careers. Quick messages to learn what they're up to or sharing the occasional memory you have with them keeps the door open in case there is some overlap in the direction you are heading. It saves you from having to write the dreaded "Remember me, I could use your help" type of message.

- **A message to a former coworker:** An easy way to begin to build the confidence to reach out to new people is by consistently reaching out to people you've already worked with. Sharing what you're up to and an interesting thing you're seeing while asking them what they're up to, and if they're seeing anything interesting is a good way to learn about what's going on in your industry. Something as simple as noting, "I hope Bob from accounts payable has learned not all phone calls need to be on speaker," keeps relationships from fizzling out.

A few years ago, I created this cheat sheet and shared it on my website. The response to the idea was overwhelming. If time is tight, commit to sending just one of the types of messages above or reserve an hour a month to go for a walk and leave voice messages for some of your weak ties. Tell them there's no rush in replying or replying at all if life is busy. Letting people know you're thinking about them is a good way to have them continue to think about you.

Committing to getting to know new people and maintaining relationships with weak ties through a well-designed system allows you to gain a significant number of people in your corner in as little as a few months. This helps make requests down the road feel less awkward as they will know that you care about them as individuals.

Networks are built by reaching out to people you admire, mastering the follow-up, and creating your tribe. But never underestimate the power of weak ties. They add strength to your network and bring innovative ideas that you might not have previously considered. They allow you to see the world from a new perspective and navigate the uncertain future by being exposed to different opportunities. Learning about the experiences and perspectives of your weak ties may serve as the inspiration you need to pursue your goals and make a positive impact in the world.

Part III

Quiet Conviction

Share What You're Learning

"I LOVE YOU, MIKE, AND I RESPECT WHAT YOU'VE DONE. BUT I can't be on your team."

I looked at the man sitting across the conference room table. "What are you talking about?" I replied, thinking he was joking as there was no way he would be saying this in front of the entire team during my first day as manager.

"I'm sorry," he said, with his normally confident eyes glued to the floor. "It's your stutter. I can't have you talking to my clients. I got kids, man. You understand, right?"

Like a lot of people who grow up with a stutter or any other trait that isn't the "norm," I got picked on and I got called names. As a kid, even while I'd often laugh along as a survival mechanism, these comments destroyed me. None of the jokes, jabs, and laughs behind my back, however, compared to the pain and rage I felt that day when a thirty-seven-year-old man whom I'd sat beside from day one on the job said he wouldn't be on my team because of my stutter.

I wish I could say I remained calm at that moment. But I didn't. I jumped out of my chair and dug into the man as if I was trying to reach China. The remainder of my team sat speechless, unable to blink. "What do you mean, you can't have me talking to your clients?" I implored. "You didn't seem to mind last Friday night when I saved your deal while you were getting wasted across the street!"

The more I laid into the man, the more he fought back. He was easily twice my size. The entirety of my body could have fit in his left shoe while still having room for a pillow. Realizing I might end up in the hospital if I kept stoking him, I told him to screw off one last time before storming out of the office, doing everything I could to hold back the tears welling in the corners of my eyes.

I don't know what was going through my head as I got in my car and drove a mile down the road to continue to curse at the world behind a Panera Bread. But it couldn't have been good. I sat in my car for over an hour thinking about what I was doing and what I was going to do. I'd been whacked across the face with the hard reality that just because I'd learned how to effectively build rapport with people, it didn't mean everyone was ready to embrace me as a leader.

VULNERABILITY IS AN ACT OF GENEROSITY

Deciding to return to the office that day was one of the most difficult decisions I'd ever made. I'd just turned twenty-five and received a significant promotion to sales manager, which should have been a momentous occasion, considering my starting point. However, my joy was short-lived due to the actions of a callous coworker. I hadn't even had the chance to enjoy the view from the top before it all came crashing down. I considered not only stepping away from the position but from the company. The awful feeling of being irate while simultaneously feeling humiliated gave me a sneak peek as to why reasonably good people sometimes do bad things. As I shakily walked back through the office doors, however, two conversations convinced me to see things through, and ultimately, played a role in opening my eyes to the type of leader I was best positioned to be.

After giving the man one last jab by telling him the next time he decides to level someone to do it in private, I went to talk to the founder and CEO of the company. I thought he'd have my back, and I was right. One of the reasons I was promoted in the first place was because I was the only person in the interview process who challenged the way of training new hires. The corporate trainer had extensive sales experience but he was new to the industry and he didn't yet know the details of the products we were selling well enough, which was my strength. I presented a hybrid approach where I would get involved earlier in their training process to ensure new hires knew not only *how* to sell but *what* they were selling. When I barged into the CEO's office, it was clear that word of what happened had already made its way up to him as he immediately said, "I'm glad you came back. I'm not sure I would have." He then sat me down and told me what I'd been able to accomplish was nothing short of incredible, he didn't promote people out of pity, and in an attempt to break the tension, he told me that my secret to success of trying not to talk very much was genius. Most importantly, he reinforced a notion growing inside of me that I had a knack for teaching.

The CEO's boost to keep moving forward helped. But I still needed to get with what was left of my team. I wasn't even six hours into my first management role and I was faced with the daunting task of trying to stop what I thought was sure to be an all-out mutiny. To my surprise, except for the man who opted out, the other team members were waiting in the conference room when I got there. Rather than having to give a sales pitch as to why they should work with me, they told me how much respect they had for me. For the next couple of hours, we talked about not only what I could do to support them, but what they could do to support me.

It was obvious to everyone in the room that I wasn't the average salesperson, let alone society's traditional definition of a leader. But rather than act like I knew what I was doing, I expressed my uncertainty and shared where I lacked confidence. Admitting I needed their help to get moving possibly more than they needed mine wasn't the conversation I thought I would have that day. But I'm glad it happened. The reason the man's comments hurt so much—apart from being a criminal offense—is because he surfaced lingering doubts I had about myself. The very words he said about not being confident in my abilities to hop on a call to save a deal going south were the very thoughts that made me hesitant to even apply for the role. If he hadn't brought it up, I wouldn't have had the courage to talk about it or ask my team for help.

Like a lot of people, growing up, the world made me believe the word "vulnerable" was synonymous with "insecure" or "weak." Due to the circumstances that day, by choosing to come back to work I was put into a position of *forced vulnerability*. I'd been exposed. Reaching for a mask wasn't an option. The support of my team opened my eyes to the fact that leaning on them and expressing my uncertainty didn't make me weak. That day marked the moment the connections I had with the other team members strengthened. By discussing my fears, my team members let me know I didn't have to go through it alone. We talked about how we could cover each other's weaknesses.

This experience allowed me to see firsthand the power of vulnerability through a new lens. The lens where we're strong enough to admit we don't have life all figured out. The lens where we're strong enough to ask for help. The lens through which we see vulnerability for what it truly is—an exercise in extreme bravery and the ultimate act of generosity.

Progress, no matter the shape or form, is the act of facing challenges and summoning the courage to push through. But it's rarely—if ever—a result of our own design. We need people and they need us. Although the conversations I had that afternoon were hard, showing up that day and every day thereafter, no matter the adversities I faced, served as a reminder to those around me of the importance of opening ourselves up to the world.

Going through this experience firsthand and internalizing this lesson at a young age has been invaluable for both my professional career and my personal life. I didn't see it playing out the way it did. But talking about my fears helped create an environment where people felt comfortable talking about their challenges and coming to me for help without feeling judged. It was one more reason for me to begin to look at my stutter and shyness as a strength. The faster people drop their guards and comfortably discuss their challenges, the faster problems get solved.

To put the icing on a day that dragged me through the gauntlet, a breakthrough moment occurred when a young team member mentioned in our meeting, "If that guy has been in sales for fifteen years and needs a manager to help talk to his clients, he may have chosen the wrong profession." He then noted that if I taught my team members well, they wouldn't need help on calls as they'd be able to handle their clients themselves.

Teaching Is Leading

Two decades have passed since that day I chose to return to work instead of pulling out of Panera's parking lot and calling it quits. I didn't get everything right in that job. Far from it. At times, I let the title and the money I was making go to my head. At that age, I also didn't know how to handle stress of that magnitude. I got frazzled juggling my deals. As a manager of a team that grew to twenty salespeople, along with eventually taking over the duties of training all new hires and continuing to serve my clients, the anxiety I experienced often went into overdrive.

The beauty of staying with difficult tasks, however, is it allows patterns to emerge that we may not otherwise see. For example, by taking the sales job in the first place, I learned I had qualities I hadn't properly recognized like being an above-average listener. The more time I spent in management, the clearer it became that the CEO of the company was right in that I lit up when teaching. Because my baseline was observing people and asking questions, I could quickly zero in on where people needed help. To compensate for not being as strong at "selling," I embraced the role of educating my team members and clients on product options and working with them to identify the best solution for their unique situations.

I didn't see myself as a leader when I started that job. When I left, I still struggled to define myself as one. I didn't fit the mold of the other managers in the office who represented the more stereotypical definition that leads with confidence and certainty. Through my experiences building small teams as an entrepreneur, leading groups of creatives, teaching at master's programs, and working as a consultant with leadership teams across the globe, I have come to understand that leaders come in various shapes and sizes. There is no one-size-fits-all approach to leadership, and no single type of leader is inherently superior to another. Some are more vocal in their approach. They set their target and motivate their team to follow their flag. Others lead from behind. They identify where their people want to go and they take on a more supportive role. Others, however, have developed the skill sets to effectively blend the two styles depending on the circumstances and the people standing in front of them.

Over the years, I've gotten better at being out in front. But it's not where I'm most effective nor is it where I'm most comfortable. Even when I'm teaching and one hundred eyes are on me, my baseline is leading from behind. Rather than design my syllabus alone, I meet with the students to better understand where they're struggling. Even if I'm not an "expert" in a particular area, turning the table and asking questions to the class creates a collaborative atmosphere where we work on addressing these pain points together. This allows people to come up with their theories, answers, and ideally, a roadmap to address their questions or areas they're struggling with, which is more motivating and empowering than being told what they should think and what they should do.

Like building connections with people, I view leadership as an act of service. However, this service is not about working *for* people, but rather working *with* them. My sole agenda is to collaborate with others to help them overcome challenges and reach their full potential. This service is akin to teaching, where the ultimate goal is for the students to become teachers and pass on their knowledge to others.

This idea of viewing leading as teaching isn't just some fluffy description. The word "lead" comes from the Latin word "duc" or "duct" which means to *lead something or someone through*. It serves as the foundation for terms like *air duct* and *aqueduct* which is to lead air or water successfully through a passage. Most poignantly, it's the foundation for the word *educate* as it's the act of leading someone toward knowledge to *produce* a desired outcome.[1]

Similar to my preconceived notions and not questioning society's definition of words like "shyness" and "vulnerability," this flip of viewing a leader as nothing more than a teacher changed everything. I struggled to claim the title "leader" but I proudly claim the title "teacher." If you want the best for people and you do what you can with what you have to enlarge them through the sharing of knowledge, experiences, or resources—whether it's a team of thousands or your little brother or sister—you're a leader.

This realization boosted my confidence and allowed me to see myself in a different light; a brighter light. Many introverted or shy people I've spoken with who are in leadership positions or make a living as public speakers or writing online nod to the notion of viewing themselves as a conduit. Their work isn't about them but rather the people they can potentially help. Although it's not always comfortable in the beginning, their drive to share what they're learning to make someone else's path easier pushes them through.

I never would have put myself in the crosshairs of giving presentations, leading seminars, facilitating groups, or even publishing articles online if my eyes hadn't opened to the fact that my work wasn't about me but rather the people who could benefit from my experiences and lessons learned. This helped take the pressure off to "perform" and better step into my voice as I was simply sharing what I had learned or was in the process of learning.

Share What You're Learning

I was once given valuable advice about the three types of experts we can learn from. The first type of expert consists of those who've successfully achieved what we aim to accomplish. The second type includes individuals who, although not as successful, have worked harder than most to excel and are capable of helping others achieve the same. The third type encompasses those who may not have broken into the top ranks but have an obsession with their area of expertise, leading them to become knowledgeable researchers who effectively share their findings with others.

Many people assume the first type—the highly successful—are the best people for us to learn from. But that's not always the case. As author and podcast host Tim Ferriss remarked, "Just because Michael Phelps is the best swimmer in the world, it doesn't mean he's the best person to teach you how to swim. There's a lot you can learn from the person who looks like they don't belong in the same pool as Phelps but came in sixth place."

There are two takeaways from Ferriss's words. First, what we learn through our unique struggles is valuable. Michael Phelps has an advantage over his competition because he has the perfect swimmer's body; his torso is longer than the average person while his legs are significantly shorter. Phelps's disproportionately large chest enables him to power himself through the water.[2] It's not a coincidence that sharks in cartoons have exaggerated chest sizes with short legs. The person who came in sixth place, however, who doesn't have the perfect swimmer's body, had to learn different skills and uncover different strengths. Maybe they don't "beat" Phelps, but by having to overcompensate in other areas, they learn how to compete through a different lens.

Second, it's not uncommon for great practitioners to teach people their way of doing things instead of digging in to identify the best way for each of us to succeed as individuals. In short, when it comes to sharing what we know, not to take anything away from Phelps as he's a tireless worker, an easier journey doesn't necessarily equate to a more effective teacher. After all, sometimes we learn more about having a successful marriage from someone who has been divorced and now has a successful relationship than someone who got it right straight off the bat.

Oftentimes, the second and third types of people have the potential to be amazing teachers, and therefore, leaders. This is because they've had to fight to improve their skill set and have benefited from more bruises and lessons learned on their journey to competency than those who may have a more natural predisposition to do something. Understanding the struggle can make them more empathetic and patient with their peers as well as more creative as they recognize there's more than one way to do something. I once asked a widely read blogger for advice on how to position an article and her reply was it'd be faster if she just did the task for me.

The man who refused to be on my team ultimately did me a massive favor as his actions helped me define the type of leader I was best positioned to be. I wasn't the type that would just tell people what to do nor was I the type that would helicopter in to put out fires as that wasn't my strength nor is it how I believe people effectively learn. Instead, I embraced digging in with people so they could put out their own fires and most importantly, guide them in a way that would allow them to uncover where in their process they were striking a match that led to deals going up in flames in the first place.

In hindsight, the man who refused to be on my team may have been the one person in the office who could have benefited the most from working with me. My young teammate was right in that the man shouldn't have needed me or anyone else to talk to his clients. His strength was getting people's attention and persuading them to work with him while my strength was retention and generating referrals. I accomplished this not through charm but by educating my clients from start to finish so they felt that the deal they were getting was a result of their own design. When smoke did arise, taking these steps made potentially difficult conversations easier as trust was there—and trust is the foundational ingredient to everything good in this world. The two of us missed out on learning from each other to strengthen our skills. I could have benefited from learning more about how he got people to his door so quickly while he could have learned more to ensure they left well-fed.

I'd become pretty good at sales but during that job, I also knew I'd never be the best nor did I have any aspiration in being the best. The feeling I got when I shared something I had fought hard to learn, however, and seeing that help someone get just 1 percent better was something I very much wanted to learn how to be the best at doing. As others began to recognize my ability to provide support, I became increasingly invested in this role. Despite not being the smoothest talker, I had an advantage in starting from a point further back than most. Combined with a burning desire to build connections and see others succeed, this enabled me to learn valuable lessons along the way. Ultimately, I used this unique perspective to help others excel, drawing on my own experiences to guide them toward their unique definition of success.

You Know Something Others Don't

Each of us has individual weaknesses, which means we also have our unique strengths. We think of our work as "a job" when in reality, every position consists of dozens of responsibilities and demands competency in an array of skills. For example, as a writer, I have to be adept in editing, storytelling, structure, researching, crafting titles, and so on. Now, combine the online element and I also have to be competent at copywriting, social media, pitching publications, self-promotion, and numerous other marketing aspects. If we substitute any other profession for writing, we'll notice a similar pattern. Success in any job often requires a range of skills and abilities. To excel, we need to surround ourselves with people who can help fill the gaps in our knowledge and abilities, and we need good teachers to guide us along the way.

My friend Sinem Günel, a twenty-five-year-old Turkish writer and entrepreneur based in Vienna, Austria, is someone I turn to regularly for guidance on how to best navigate my online work. Some people have larger audiences and earn more money than Sinem. But since she began writing a few years ago, she's been documenting her journey and helping those younger than she as well as those twice her age to set up an online business in a way that resonates with me. Though she says she's a writer and entrepreneur, Sinem is first and foremost an educator. The best part about Sinem is she doesn't pretend to have all the answers. Her forte is helping people a step or two behind her to gain the skills and confidence to ultimately surpass her. As a result of this sharing mindset—and being in the weeds with the people she works with—she's built a reputation as a trustworthy source at a young age.

Sinem's not the only one. During any given week, I'm working with two groups of people. The first group consists of those who proactively get involved in their office by offering to mentor new hires or host workshops in areas that interest them, or you can find them online sharing their knowledge and experiences. The second group of people are simply those who don't make that effort. It shouldn't come as a surprise the first group is flooded with opportunities compared to the second group. Rather than dream of one day giving a TED Talk, they're making the effort each day to share the content that may one day lead them to be asked to give a TED Talk.

We live in a world where technology and therefore the ways we work, live, and communicate are changing at warp speed. The knowledge that we often take for granted, such as learning to use a new app that has improved our organization or exploring the nuances of effective writing, can be extremely valuable to those seeking to improve their own skills in these areas. My friend—and now marketing thought leader on both LinkedIn and X—Jon Brosio has built a solid reputation by sharing what he's learning about how to write persuasive copy. He'll be the first to tell you he's not reinventing the wheel but rather pulling together valuable ideas and resources he's learning on his journey as he develops his own theories and best practices. Like Sinem, this makes him extremely likable. They understand the wisdom of musician Drake's words, "People like you more when you are working toward something, not when you have it."

We are spoiled for choice today regarding how and where we can join the conversation. If making long-form YouTube videos isn't your thing, TikTok is an option. If video, in general, isn't your thing, you can write long-form articles on your blog or on platforms like Medium or Substack. If you aren't confident in your article writing ability, you have X and LinkedIn to share short messages as you build your communication and connection muscles. If none of this is your thing or makes you uncomfortable, you can share what you like from people you admire or messages that resonate with you and slowly add in your perspectives. The important thing is that you start. This is because sharing is a magnet.

SHARING IS A MAGNET

The beauty of sharing what we know—and are learning—is that we don't need to learn new material; we just have to focus on our presentation. When I moved to Spain, I continued my pattern of mentorship, just as I had in my previous sales job. Given my experience with sales and interviewing, I volunteered to assist expats in finding work at the training center where I received certification to teach English. At first, I provided one-on-one sessions, but as my confidence grew, I progressed to giving monthly seminars and small-group workshops. Although I only taught English for a few years, I continued to offer these seminars, using repetition to refine my material and build my confidence in presenting to larger groups. In the end, I had presented to well over a thousand people. Not content to stop there, I started a blog to share the material from these seminars and to further develop my writing skills.

I'm convinced that making this continual effort, combined with learning how to effectively share my story—which we'll dive into in the next principle, "Own Your Story"—are the leading reasons why I've never had to market my work or look for clients in close to a decade of being self-employed. Rather than push my services on people, I pull them into my world through relatability and generosity. Due to having a desire to see each client win, the referrals haven't stopped rolling in.

I reached out to both Jon Brosio and Sinem Günel as well as hundreds of other up-and-coming creators making the sizable waves they're making today as I was drawn to their energy. The confidence and improvement in communication skills I've seen these people gain over the years have been incredible to witness. Regardless if their message takes off, they stand taller and the chances of connecting with the people they admire increase exponentially. This is because they've chosen to enter the arena and people tend to prioritize making time for those who are making an effort to lift up others more than those who aren't.

We don't even need to be experts with decades of experience to begin to reap the benefits of being a "sharer." We just need to be consistently curious and generous and have a strong desire to do good by others. Opening ourselves up to the world and saying, "This is what I'm interested in, and here are my takes and experiences on topics that matter to me," can be petrifying. God knows I've been there and at times, after posting more than three hundred stories and articles online, I'm still there. The fear of judgment from others is real. We're going to be diving into how to build our boldness muscle in principle 11, "Be Bold in the Moments That Matter." But for starters, remind yourself that the things we're scared of are often the things we care about the most. We don't want to fail or be made fun of when we take our shot in these areas. But if I've learned anything since taking that sales job, it's that for every person who refuses to be a part of our team, there are a dozen people who respect us for having the courage to put ourselves out into the world.

That's the beauty of sharing.

It's an invitation.

But it's not only an invitation to connect with other people and potentially help them on their way. It's also an invitation to better connect with ourselves. This is because when we proactively share what we're learning, we gain the confidence to begin to share who we are. And when we share who we are—and learn how to properly express our story—we not only step into our voice, we begin to own it.

PRINCIPLE 10

Own Your Story

SOME PEOPLE DREAM EARLY IN THEIR LIVES OF HAVING KIDS AND starting a family.

I was not one of those people.

The moment I saw my wife, Laia, holding a pregnancy test with the positive results written all over her smiling face, rather than shed tears of joy like you sometimes see in the movies, I gave her a limp hug before sheepishly asking, "Are you sure?"

As the days passed and the due date loomed closer, I thought for sure all the fears running through my head would subside, but they didn't. While Laia's glow intensified, the more stressed I became. One minute, I'd be worried I wouldn't be able to provide for my family, and the next, I'd convince myself I'd have to put my dreams on hold *for the next eighteen years*. Most of all, I was petrified that I wouldn't be a good dad, and paralyzed by the notion that my son would inherit some of my traits.

"What if he stutters like me?"

"What if he's stupid like me?"

"What if he's damaged like me?"

The shame I experienced for allowing this internal chatter to dominate my narrative instead of giving Laia the support she deserved was hard to reconcile in my head. But rather than listen to Laia and slow down and work to get to the root of these insecurities, I did the opposite. I threw myself into anything and everything I could think of to gain some semblance of control and financial security. It got to the point that during the third trimester, I landed on the idea of selling koozies. Why I believed flogging two-dollar pieces of neoprene to keep people's beers cold in Barcelona was the answer to all of my problems still eludes me.

Not surprisingly, the faster I ran, the more lost I felt.

Tick-tock.

Tick-tock.

But that early morning when our son Liam finally graced us with his presence, after the medical staff joked with me one too many times that they'd include me on their rounds of people to check on, something magical happened.

Minutes after Liam was born, the nurses passed him to me so they could help Laia get more comfortable. Like all babies, he came into the world upset he'd just been taken from his cozy home. I'm sure seeing a bunch of people twenty times his size wielding scissors didn't help to alleviate his unease. But the second he got nestled in my arms, he looked up at me, and when our eyes met, for the first time in his short life, he stopped crying.

This silent embrace and game of *who can go the longest without blinking* only lasted a few minutes before the hysterics kicked back in.

But that was long enough.

When I went to place Liam back in his mom's arms, for the first time since Laia let me know she was pregnant, I smiled and meant it.

The Journey Home

I never would have guessed the spark I needed in my career would come in the form of starting a family. But overnight, my priorities shifted. Before Liam's arrival, I'd bounced around for several years trying to find the work I was meant to be doing. But being that my purpose was now staring at me in the face each morning as I changed his diapers, rather than continue to prioritize figuring out what I wanted to do, I finally followed Laia's advice to hit pause and zero in on the person I was.

Both Laia and Liam deserved better than the way I'd been operating.

They made me finally realize *I deserved* better than the way I'd been operating.

I needed to get to the bottom of these lingering insecurities that the news of becoming a father triggered to better rewrite the story I told myself that I was destined to be a failure and walking punchline.

So over the following months, I did just that. I worked enough to pay the bills teaching English as it allowed for a flexible schedule, and when I wasn't caring for Liam, I dug in to get to the heart of my identity and own the journey I'd been on.

I met with a therapist to voice these feelings of inadequacy. We hit rewind and explored the moments I felt embarrassed, scared, or downright terrified, starting with my earliest memories through to the present moment. As daily homework, in addition to writing about my feelings, thoughts, and experiences, I gave myself the space to really think about the values I wanted to uphold, ordering them by importance to create a north star for how I wanted to show up in the world.

The words came pouring out of me.

But I didn't stop with how *I* viewed myself. I also spoke with my family and I reached out to friends from childhood through college to get their take on what I was like when I was younger. Their comments ranged from quiet and shy to traits I didn't see in myself at the time, like having a quirky sense of humor, being highly creative, and possessing the surprising ability to turn into a lawyer when I wanted something. Most of all, I was told I was sensitive, and time and time again, people shared how much they appreciated how empathetic I was.

It didn't come quickly, and it wasn't always fun, but slowly but surely, the life dots I'd collected began to connect. The very qualities that other people led with when describing the aspects they most admired in me were the very traits I was most proud of when writing alone about my journey.

Empathetic. Creative. Sensitive. Quirky sense of humor. Vulnerable. A breakthrough moment occurred when I put all of these words onto one page and identified all the good things and great people these qualities had brought into my life.

And since that experience, I haven't missed a single day of writing.

It's my chance to be honest with myself.

It's my chance to take a step back to better process the world and my role in it.

It's my chance to better define how to best love and support my family, and most of all, myself.

When I began to share my insecurities, mistakes made, and moments of extreme embarrassment on my blog a year later as a way to begin to step out into the world without a mask, I never would have imagined the response. A few people warned me that being so open would be kryptonite for my career. But over time, the opposite happened. Rather than being a career killer, sharing who I am became my life accelerator.

Not only did many recent college graduates who shared similar feelings and thoughts of inadequacy begin to reach out to let me know how much my messages helped, but seasoned executives and entrepreneurs also began to express interest in working with me as they saw a lot of themselves in my story.

These messages and opportunities caught me off guard, but looking back, it makes perfect sense. Waking up each day and working with people to grow their confidence and better own their stories is *my* story. I've lived it. It's all I've ever known. And although it took thirty-eight years and a seven-pound human to inspire me to do the work on myself, for myself, I wouldn't want it any other way. I needed time to uncover who I was and I needed time to discover the people I was best positioned to support. Plus, growing up, it's not exactly like I had a lot of people telling me my career purpose was obvious: "You should help people better express themselves!"

However, before we move into the journey of discovering ways to own our story, it's important to understand what the concept of "story" means in today's world.

Honesty Is the World's Most Valuable Currency

The simplest definition of a story is a character faces a challenge and they're willing to risk or sacrifice everything, even their life, to overcome it.

The word "storytelling," however, gets tossed around a lot today and has an array of interpretations. Depending on the resources you pick up or the type of teachers you have, you may view storytelling as a tactic to drum up business. Many people encourage us to write with a specific audience in mind. To share our story as a way to build a personal brand and for businesses to embrace storytelling to show consumers the human side of their business. To shade our messaging in a way that says, "Hey friend, I'm like you. You should get to know me. I can help!" Some marketing professionals and copywriters encourage us to embrace tactics like "agitate," "exaggerate," and "twist the knife" to ensure the reader's "pain points" are "amplified" to the point they have no other recourse but to click on our offer.

There's a place for this type of storytelling, the kind that's geared toward persuading people to follow, your flag. But before we get to that point, we first have to define which flag we want people to follow, as learning how to persuade people prior to having a firm grip on your values can lead to dangerous results.

The kind of storytelling I'm talking about is rooted in the art of self-expression. The type of storytelling that has existed since the dawn of civilization. The type of storytelling where the only tactic is not having a tactic as you're simply noting your unique human experience.

This kind of storytelling may not lead to the kind of mass appeal that sharing your story with an agenda and audience in mind can earn. But when your honest story filled with bumps and beauty and warts and wonder does connect with someone, worlds collide. Worlds where people don't just want to follow your flag. Worlds where, instead, people are inspired to take your hand and carry the flag with you.

This is because we all have unique drivers, but one red thread that runs through humanity is that every one of us craves the power of choice.

The choice to make our own decisions.

The choice to decide what's best for us.

The choice to decide whose story we want to be a part of.

This means your job when telling your story is not to try to push your agenda onto people but rather to create the space for others to choose if they want to join your story. Put simply, rather than worry about what people want to hear, we first root our story in exactly who we are, what we've experienced, and what we want to say. We treat our story like a piece of art—our unique expression of our unique human experience. Like Rick Rubin, famed producer of many artists that can't be replicated, said in his book

The Creative Act: A Way of Being, "Part of the process of letting go is releasing any thoughts of how you or your piece will be received. When making art, the audience comes last."

This should give you extreme confidence.

This is because this kind of storytelling demands you be yourself. It entails that you first write your story for an *audience of none*.

One of the biggest challenges we face today is deciphering the smoke from the substance, the fact from the fiction, the artificial from the beating heart. By sharing your unique human experience, it's the honesty that creates the market.

So the big question becomes, "What is your honest story?" The best way to begin to unpack that is by collecting the defining moments of your life, including both the brutal and the beautiful, because inside those experiences hides glimpses of the person you are as well as the one you want to become.

DISSECT YOUR PAST TO BETTER WRITE YOUR FUTURE

If I learned anything throughout my experience of going on a deep dive into who I am and what I stand for, it's that life is about pattern recognition, and it becomes much easier to connect your life dots if you make the effort to continually collect them. However, one way to catch up on this is by revisiting the questions I shared in Principle 4 that I send to my students before the start of our first class and expanding upon them.

- What is one of the defining moments of your life (good or bad)?

- What is your "why" or motivator for doing what you do?

- Who is one person or one piece of advice that has helped you on your way?

Though basic, these questions get us thinking about not only these moments and realizations but also the circumstances around them. They also often reveal some sort of transformation or "state change" that demonstrates a before and after—moving from lost to found, unemployed to employed, overweight to in shape, hopeless to hopeful, in the dark to enlightened, and so on. You can't go wrong by starting with a basic structure like, "I was there, and now I'm here. Here's what happened," when beginning to craft your story before filling in the details.

For example, a twenty-five-year-old former student from Lebanon didn't see any of the defining moments of his life as "story-worthy." But by asking what motivated him to move to Barcelona to get his master's degree in project management, a gold nugget insight revealed itself. In 2020, he quit his engineering job for a reputable construction firm to volunteer for the United Nations after the August 4 explosions occurred in his hometown of Beirut. Growing up surrounded by destruction, he chose to sacrifice his comfort and well-being to utilize his skill set in construction to rebuild his city for the collective good. Here's a crystallized version of where we landed after ironing out the details of his experiences:

> My passions are community and construction. This is because I grew up in a place where destruction was the norm. When the explosions occurred in Beirut in 2020, I quit my engineering job to volunteer my services for the UN. I'm pursuing my master's in Barcelona to improve my skill set to ultimately return home to rebuild my city stronger than it was before.

This is his story and his alone. In a few sentences, it explains why he does what he does as well as his values, which are often an integral part of a compelling personal story. Before taking the time to think about his experiences, he didn't think he had a story, yet with a little prying, it turns out he has one that defines the human experience and transcends borders.

The same goes for my friend Alba Mihaj. On the first day of class, Alba made it very clear she would not be sharing her story, and each time we met, I was convinced I wasn't reaching her. During the final fifteen minutes of our last class, however, she pulled me aside and said, "I need to do this."

In one of the most beautiful moments I've ever witnessed, Alba demonstrated that she was not only paying attention, but outside of class, she was putting her learning into action. From the moment she began telling her story, she had the entire class hanging on to her every word for the duration of her ten-minute talk. She shared that a year prior she lost her superpower when her father suddenly passed away. He was her rock. Her best friend. She felt utterly lost without him. With not a single dry eye in the room, she explained that moving to Barcelona and pursuing her master's was her first step in trying to find her superpowers again. In the end, her bravery and raw vulnerability inspired thirty students from all over the globe to end our time together in a group hug.

Seeing this transformation and watching Alba step into her voice was beyond inspiring. But she didn't stop there. A week after she shared her story, she messaged me to let me know she was about to tell it again, only this time at an open-mic night in front of a room of strangers. When she landed a job that she really wanted a month later, she credited her newfound confidence and the fact she brought her full self to the interview as the reason she got selected. Alba volunteering to give a guest talk to a group of my students on the first day of a new course is an experience I'll always carry with me.

When crafting your own story, maybe the light bulb moments don't pop out immediately. It's amazing, though, what experiences and lessons do arise once we get them onto the page and begin to discuss them with others in a safe environment. This is because our story is already inside of us and it just needs a little coaching and coaxing to get uncovered and communicated in a way that we can proudly stand behind.

DESIGN A TIMELINE OF YOUR LIFE

I'm a big believer that the best way to start something—any-thing—is by starting small. The three questions asked earlier can be helpful as they demand thinking about just one moment, your primary motivator, and one piece of advice or influential relationship.

An effective way to add to these themes that have helped both myself and my students is creating a timeline of your life, which is an exercise that is often used in self-awareness, team-building, and creativity courses. Countless times, as either a participant or a moderator of this activity, I've witnessed people not only draw deeper meaning from experiences they initially deemed as incon-sequential but also build connections with others as it bypasses small talk and is rooted in getting to the heart of who people are. Similar to a margarita pizza, it's a classic exercise for a reason: it works, it's easy to prepare, and it allows for additional toppings.

- Take a piece of paper, turn it horizontally, and draw a line across the middle from one end to the other. You can do this on your computer, but I recommend first completing this exercise with a pen and paper as the act itself will slow you down.

- Start from the day you were born and identify any events that have had an impact on your life up until now—per-sonal and professional, big and small, good or bad. These initial entries could include events or milestones such as graduating from high school or college, starting a new job, moving to a new city or country, reaching a big goal, falling short, romantic relationships, meeting your best friend, experiencing a loss or health issue, and so on.

- Once your first draft is done, since the exercise is brewing in your head, revisit it a day or two later, and then also a week or two later, while asking if you missed anything.

- Last, consider making it a breathing document. Our lives, and therefore our story, are a continual work in progress.

Taking the time to do this exercise—and continue to revisit it—will allow you to gain new perspectives regarding specific events while being able to see certain periods of your life "in context" and the lessons they ultimately taught you. By taking the time to reflect, patterns and themes will also arise, allowing you to dive deeper into these areas that have the potential to reveal why you hold certain values.

One thing I like to do is to take this exercise a step further by designing it around specific themes and digging deeper into the details of these experiences. These could include the following areas.

- **Create a timeline solely of your defining career moments.** This could entail getting more specific regarding your thoughts and feelings around challenges you've faced, milestones you've reached, projects you've worked on, key decisions you've made, or relationships you've formed for each year you've worked.

- **Create a timeline of your defining relationships**. This may consist of intimate relationships or friendships which allows you to zero in on key lessons you've learned from these people and the experiences you've shared. Revisiting old photos, emails, text messages, and social media posts can help to iron out the time frames while serving as a spark to remind you of the circumstances.

- **Create a timeline of the moments you got seriously pissed off.** It's amazing what we uncover when we sit with the moments that made us angry. If you dig a little, you may find that the actions or words of someone else or a wrong you want to right in the world helps you uncover your values. For example, being curious and kind are two of my leading values. This is because I know what it feels like to be treated on the opposite end of the spectrum.

You can even use this structure to map out what you were doing, where you were, and who you were with on each of your birthdays as the chances are good that the circumstances changed. The options are limitless. By mapping out the most beautiful moments of my life, the most brutal, as well as moments where I experienced a turning point, you get the content and stories for this book.

Take your time with these exercises. By sitting with these experiences and asking follow-up questions regarding the circumstances, the emotions they evoked, and the lessons they imparted, valuable stories that are hidden in plain sight will begin to reveal themselves.

For the majority of my life, I thought I didn't have a story and I sure didn't think I had one that people would care about. It took some time, but by carving out space to get to know myself while continuing to explore the world and my role in it, I realized I am story-worthy.

When people ask me, "So what's your story?" or the dreaded, "Tell me about yourself," I respond with a variation of the following statement:

I grew up shy with a severe stutter and I struggled to build relationships. To overcome my fears and grow my confidence, I pursued a sales job and I now help people who share similar challenges to create connections with people and own their stories.

In a matter of ten seconds (well, maybe twelve if I get hung up), people not only learn what I do but why I do it. This answer shows the journey I've been on while demonstrating one of my core values—sharing what I've learned to make someone else's journey easier. Most importantly, it's honest. No slick marketing or clever copy is needed. I can confidently share my story because I've lived my story.

You're Worth Getting to Know

I'm forever grateful for Laia, Liam, and our latest addition, Luc. I've learned many valuable lessons about how to lead a meaningful life from the three of them. But few are more important than this one: good things happen when we stop.

Each day, no matter what I have going on and no matter how fast life is moving, I reserve, at a minimum, thirty minutes for myself—the equivalent of less than two percent of the day. Half of the time I use this break from the world to just breathe, and the other half, to note my thoughts, feelings, and experiences.

We live in a hectic world that shows little signs of slowing down. When we go online, the speed only intensifies and it's hard not to think we're the only people who don't have life figured out. However, while everyone else is running, choose to be the person who sits on a park bench and enjoys a delicious peach from time to time. Carry a notepad with you and each day and take note of the challenges you are facing, the moments that light you up, and your thoughts and feelings around these experiences.

To step into your big story, it sure helps if you take note of your daily experiences. Seemingly mundane events like getting ready to meet with a new client, moving to a new town, transitioning between jobs, or making a new friend possess a relatable quality, with the potential to unveil moments of self-discovery and newfound understanding of the world.

Your story may not provide all the answers, but it enriches the ongoing conversation both with yourself and others.

Your story is forever work.

You're worth getting to know.

And you may find that the more you dig into your experiences and see how much you've already overcome, you gain the courage to be bold in the moments that matter.

Be Bold in the Moments That Matter

THE WOMAN SAT AT HER KITCHEN TABLE, STARING AT THE FOUR names laid out in front of her. Her hand was shaking. Despite being seventy-eight years old, her heart raced with the same intensity as it did when she had her first crush as a teenager.

Months earlier, while walking the Camino de Santiago, a five-hundred-mile trek across northern Spain, the woman met a man. It seemed like a typical friendly encounter with a stranger, one of many she'd had since arriving in the country. The conversation lasted only a few minutes, and when they parted ways, they didn't even exchange names.

But after the woman made her way back home to Norway once her journey was over, she couldn't stop thinking about the man. There was something about him. She couldn't quite put her finger on exactly why his face flashed before her closed eyes as she lay in bed alone at night, but she knew she had to see him again.

When she'd planned the trip, meeting someone new was the last thing on her mind. She'd decided to go on the walk to come to grips with the passing of her husband a few years prior. It was her way of reentering the world after her paralyzing loss. Yet, again and again, she kept replaying the exchange she had with the comfortable stranger she'd met. That is, until one day she decided to do something about it.

Not knowing where else to turn, she called the office of the Camino de Santiago and shared the whole story. She explained how she met a man during the walk. She said she didn't have much information about him, but she knew he was from the Netherlands. She laughed when she admitted she didn't even know the man's name.

The woman knew the odds were against her as most organizations have strict rules about passing along the personal information of other people. As luck would have it, the woman she spoke with had a soft spot for the story. It took some digging, but by the time the call ended, the woman had the names and mailing addresses of four Dutchmen who finished the walk around the same time as she did.

All the days she'd spent dreaming about the man had suddenly become very real. She couldn't believe it. "What do I do now?" she asked herself. "What do I even say?" But a few days later, after pacing her house with the names of the four men in hand, she hatched a plan. Immediately, she sat down and spent the rest of the evening writing out four identical Christmas cards to each of the men.

Three years later, while my dad was walking the Camino de Santiago to straighten out the twists of a recent big life event of his own, he stopped in a café a few kilometers short of Leon, Spain. He pulled up a seat at the bar. He noticed an elderly couple to his right. He nodded and said hello. After sharing a few glasses of wine, my father asked the two of them how they met.

The couple smiled. Then the man explained that one day while going through his mail, he found a letter from a stranger.

IF YOU DON'T ASK, YOU DON'T GET

Sometimes when I'm feeling stuck, I imagine the woman in this story, sitting alone at her kitchen table, thinking about the man she'd met. I imagine her picking up the phone and then putting it back down again, wondering if the whole plan was absurd. But then I imagine her thinking, "What have I got to lose?" and slowly dialing the number to the information center and stumbling her way through asking for help. I then envision her writing out the fourth letter with the same level of care as she did the first. I can practically feel her heart pounding in her chest. I can see the lines on her face shifting when she finally looks down at her mail one day and sees the man's name staring back at her.

When I think about the woman's actions on the day she decided to lead with boldness, I'm reminded that we'll never get what we want out of life if we don't summon the strength to ask for it.

How many days do we waste living in a state of hesitation because we're scared of being rejected?

How many times have we sat paralyzed thinking of the countless ways our potential dreams could go wrong?

How many opportunities have passed us by because we chose to give more power to our excuses than our possibilities?

Stories from people like the elderly woman reinforce the notion that I don't want to live my life in a constant state of hesitation. Instead, I choose forward motion.

Maybe this means you'll have to send a thousand letters. Maybe you'll get rejected, and it will hurt. Maybe you'll find out that what you thought you wanted isn't actually what you want, and you have to change course and start again. It's all part of the deal. But when you default to taking action, you open yourself to a life of opportunities, stories, and relationships that can bring great joy and meaning into your life.

Use Your Past to Fuel Your Present

A part of me wishes I was more like the people who say they don't have any regrets. I have loads of regrets. The ones that stick with me the most, though, aren't from the times something didn't pan out or I made a mistake that could have been avoided. Instead, they're from the times I didn't dare to try in the first place, the times when I succumbed to fear or gave more weight to the opinions of others over prioritizing my own internal signal. It's taken me a long time to learn this, but as long as we're alive and capable, regrets aren't even regrets—they're reminders.

Reminders that we can still make the time.

Reminders that the choice is ours.

Reminders that change is possible.

We may get one shot at life. But during our lives, we have the opportunity to take countless shots. It's our obligation to ourselves and those around us to permit ourselves to make our own green lights in life. An argument can be made that it's selfish not to as we're robbing the world of our potential if we don't summon the courage to go after what we want.

I have many stories where despite my fears, I acted with boldness when it mattered. Times when I stood up when I desperately wanted to stay seated. Moments when I spoke up and said, "This isn't right!" Moments when I said to hell with it, I have to be me. These instances didn't always pan out. Some of them left me emotionally bruised, mentally battered, and financially broke.

After growing my confidence in my first sales job, I took everything I had and spent everything I'd earned trying my hand at property development in Central America. It ended horribly. I got screwed over by a guy I considered family. In the span of one phone call, I lost everything I'd worked so hard to achieve—including my sanity and newly found self-esteem—due to one man's decisions and an archaic legal system. I felt ashamed that at the age of thirty I had to return to my hometown with nothing to show for myself except a story of how I'd lost $250,000 because a man changed the deed of my house to his name and sold it out from under me. I thought for sure this loss would be my demise and I was convinced the black stain would remain present throughout the entirety of my career. Looking back, however, I take great pride in making that decision.

This is because even though I missed, I took the shot I wanted to take.

Though the future was uncertain as I was out of a job and I didn't have any money, two years later, once I was done feeling sorry for myself and drowning my sorrows in any bar that would put up with me, I rolled the dice again. This time, though, I packed my life into a backpack and bought a one-way ticket to Barcelona, Spain.

I knocked on doors for six months before I began to receive the yeses I needed. All the perceived rejections and supposed failures I'd experienced culminated one day when I met the one person in the world I was supposed to meet. A woman who was busy collecting her own moments of being bold in the moments that mattered for her life to make sense.

While I was trying to get my footing in my first sales job, the woman decided to move to Dublin from a small town in Catalunya to learn English. It was a dream of hers to travel and live abroad. Despite being the epitome of shyness, she boarded a plane and fought to find work at a convenience store selling six-packs and lottery tickets to pay her bills and practice English. Once this adventure was complete, she boarded another plane. And then another, crisscrossing the globe and then back again with a backpack and a friend.

A decade later, when we met, I'd overstayed my visa in Spain and wasn't allowed to live or work legally in the country. Despite this, one of my close friends, Jamie Cruickshank, referred me to an interview for a job giving a presentation and negotiation seminar for the Catalan government. "There's no way I'll get hired for that," I said. "Plus, I'll get deported if anyone finds out I'm not legal." But instead of agreeing with me, Jamie replied, "Just go for it, mate. You'll have to leave anyway if you run out of money."

I thought the interview would be a waste of time. I'd already gone through dozens only to be told I'd be hired if I was a European resident. But as I headed for the door, the agency owner stopped me and said, "Screw it. You're the best person for this job. We'll find a way to make it work."

On the first day of the seminar, that same woman introduced herself. She told me she was petrified of speaking in public but she signed up for the training anyway because she thought it would be good for her confidence.

All these twists and turns and risks and gambles led the two of us to stand outside of her office one day after the seminar was over. She later told me from the moment I began sharing my story she found me interesting. She liked how I didn't pretend to have all the answers. She liked how I had the stones to start my life over in a new country. She was intrigued by how a guy who stuttered got into the communication world. Before meeting me, she'd never had the courage to ask anyone out before. But that changed on that overcast October day. Eleven months later, that same woman, Laia, and I got married at a small ceremony surrounded by our closest friends and family.

The most meaningful things in our lives become that way because we put work into them. The times we choose to take a chance. Our sweat, our tears, our fears, our dreams, and our lessons learned all get rolled up into a handful of decisions that ultimately define our lives.

The things that matter most aren't given to us.

The things that matter most are created by taking daily action and being bold in the moments that matter.

Collect Your Moments of Boldness

When most people think of boldness or bravery, they often envision someone fearless, like a bulletproof superhero immune to fear. Maybe some people like this do exist. But I highly doubt it as fear, uncertainty, and doubt are feelings that define the human condition. Some people may experience fewer of these feelings than others or do a better job hiding or managing them. But regardless, these feelings are experienced. This means that acting bravely or leading with boldness isn't about fighting to rid yourself of these feelings entirely, but rather acknowledging them and making the commitment to act anyway.

I often view myself as the opposite of brave. My palms sweat when meeting new people. My heart races when I begin teaching a new class. I still can't get my left leg to stop twitching so damn much when giving an online presentation. But at the same time, I've also traveled the world, often on my own. I've moved to new countries without any friends or opportunities waiting for me and fought like hell in an attempt to make it work. I've put my fears aside after being humiliated and made the choice countless times to continue to show up.

Put simply, I am brave.

The good news is that so are you.

You've made it this far, which means you've already overcome many circumstances that challenged you and environments that scared you. Rather than wait for other people to praise your bravery, validate your brave actions yourself. Catalog your experiences. Create your own "Boldness" or "Bravery" list of all the little moments you acted with courage and the big moments when your back was up against the wall and you lived to tell the tale.

Included in this exercise, make sure to collect the moments you had the courage to say no to something that went against your values and the times you had the courage to ask for help. We may not view these actions as brave since we often feel weak or uncertain when doing them, but they're the epitome of bravery. Saying no and asking for help means you're courageous enough to stand up for yourself and admit you're not okay and could use a shoulder or a hand.

Collect your moments of bravery, no matter how small you think they may be. Remind yourself that every time nerves course through your body, you're being bold because you're pushing through what you feel is uncomfortable. You can even take these notes and put them in a "Holy Shit!" jar consisting of all the times you couldn't believe you had the courage to do something. This simple act serves as a powerful reminder on the days you don't feel like moving forward because of how far you've already come.

Although this fear may never disappear entirely—nor should we want it to as emotions are what give the world color and our experiences deeper meaning—by continuing to show up, this discomfort can begin to loosen its grip as you start to feel a little bit more comfortable standing on the edges.

One thing you don't have to do, however, is run head-first into what scares you. Instead, you can choose to slowly build your boldness muscle by taking tiny steps of daily bravery.

TAKE TINY STEPS OF DAILY BRAVERY

No matter the titles I've collected or the accolades I've received, not a day goes by when my palms don't sweat. Every time I open my mouth and I'm asked to repeat what I just said, I turn into a bright red tomato. I show up anyway. It's my superpower. Showing up is how I demonstrate I care.

But one thing I don't do is show up and take daily jumps without first taking a lot of little strategic hops. I learned the value of taking one small step at a time during my first sales job. During the first few months, rather than potentially botching a big deal, I was instructed to call old leads that weren't likely to pan out. The mindset of making "Just try!" the goal meant I had nothing to lose. Rather than celebrate only deals we closed, every Friday afternoon we congratulated each other on how many times we picked up the phone. In the process, I learned that confidence—and also respect from the right people—aren't only earned by getting things right, they're also gained by choosing to be the type of person who tries.

I followed this same strategy when I began writing. Prior to publishing articles in public, I practiced the craft in private and elicited help from people who knew more than I did. When I ran my first article, I was nervous, but I hit publish anyway because the overriding feeling was excitement as I knew I'd put in the work. I've published upward of three hundred articles and each of them started by choosing to write one word, and then another, and then another.

If your goal is to write, rather than putting pressure on yourself to publish daily, make a commitment to write one sentence a day. The chances are good that some days, you won't want to stop once your sentence is written. If your goal is to get in front of people you admire, maybe your tiny act of daily bravery could be committing to simply saying hello to one stranger a day. If your goal is to improve your public speaking, embrace the habit of recording yourself for three minutes a day. No one has to see it. You can talk about anything. You make the rules. Read a passage from a book or record one thing you learned the previous day. The important thing, no matter what your goals are, is to begin.

Since many of my fears are speaking-based, I make a point to make small talk with waitstaff and cashiers, call at least one friend a day, and organize after-school football games with my kids' friends because it attracts a few other parents which leads to lightweight, upbeat conversations. I'm not always comfortable or confident when doing these things. But by doing so, I know I'm building my boldness muscle so I'm better prepared when the stakes are raised or my values get pressure tested.

Rather than be reactive when life tests you, get in your reps by proactively practicing tiny acts of boldness to build your bravery muscle. When approaching something that scares you, ask yourself: "What do I need so that I can act with more bravery?"

CHIP AWAY AT YOUR FEARS BY EMBRACING THE "AAA" FRAMEWORK

Throughout the spring of 2022, once again, my sanity got tested. Every time I picked up the phone, I received bad news. On top of losing a work contract due to an issue with my residency status in Spain and trying to juggle two kids while my wife and I began packing in preparation for our move to a new town, a family member was diagnosed with a serious health issue and because of COVID-19, I couldn't travel to see them.

During this time, however, I was referred to a self-care expert, Jeanette Bronée, regarding helping out with her book, *The Self-Care Mindset*.[1] When expressing my concerns about accepting the offer, Jeanette gently responded, "My book is about the tools I teach to reclaim agency and better navigate fear, uncertainty, and doubt. The reason I got into this work is due to losing my parents in the span of a year to cancer at the age you are now. Maybe working with me is just what you need."

By working with Jeanette, I received a six-month master class on developing the courage to care for yourself. One of the many valuable tools Jeanette teaches that stuck with me is a framework she designed called the "AAA Framework: Acknowledge, Accept, Ask."

The first step, rather than running or trying to suppress our emotions, we should *acknowledge* what we are feeling. The second step is to *accept* the circumstances and our feelings for what they are while reminding ourselves we aren't broken or weak for having certain emotions, just human. Last, the third step serves as a spark to *ask* ourselves, "What do I need so that I can . . . ?"

As a people-pleaser, and especially a client-pleaser, I struggle with speaking up when I'm feeling stuck or lacking confidence. But rather than pushing through when times got particularly stressful while working with Jeanette, she encouraged me to use her tools against her. By acknowledging the emotions I was feeling, accepting the reality in front of me, and then asking what I needed to confidently push through, I felt more in control and communicated with Jeanette what I needed. Sometimes this came in the form of telling her I had to hit pause for a few days so I could be more present when handling personal matters. Other times, it came in the form of telling Jeanette I needed help and illicited the support of my trusted editor buddy Stephen Moore so we stayed on schedule. In the end, Jeanette coached me through hitting her deadline. Talk about micro.

Give this exercise a shot. No matter if you're facing a personal or professional challenge, the reminder to pause, acknowledge what you're feeling, accept the circumstances for what they are, and ask what you need to begin to reclaim agency is extremely effective. For example, if you too get rattled speaking in public, you can use AAA this way:

- Acknowledge: "I'm feeling uncertain and I'm scared I'll screw up and make a fool of myself."
- Accept: "I'm lacking confidence right now, but this is important to me and my feelings make me human."
- Ask: "What do I need so that I can feel more confident?"

Maybe the next step you could take is to record yourself saying only the parts of your presentation you already feel are strong to regain momentum. Or maybe it could be writing out your presentation again to have the flow stick better in your head. Or maybe it could be calling a trusted friend who gives you the space to express how you're feeling and get feedback on your work. This last point of calling a friend is particularly helpful. We don't have to—nor do we need to—face our fears alone. As stated previously, "Help" is often the bravest word we can say. By doing so, you begin to realize that having the courage to lean on others leads to deeper relationships as the friendships that mean the most are forged by helping each other overcome challenges. Not only that, but taking this step can lead to better outcomes as two heads and hearts are stronger than one.

Jeanette's framework is a cheat code for helping hard things feel a little easier. If it helps, do what I do and pin the letters "AAA" and the question "What do I need so that I can . . . ?" to your office wall. Remind yourself of Jeanette's wisdom that the things we worry about are also the things we care about. This act can help flip your self-talk from being a "worrier" to being a "carer." And if all else fails, sit down and write the best-case scenario for taking action on your dreams and the worst-case scenarios, before prioritizing the former and lighting a match to the latter.

Make a List of the Worst Case Scenarios, and Then Burn It

The best part about getting older—assuming you accept the gift of perspective—is patterns begin to emerge. One of the most valuable ones I've recognized is the times when I've felt stupid, embarrassed, or even ashamed are also the times that taught me a valuable lesson, and in some cases, over time, they even rectified themselves.

As described previously, my peers and even one of my teachers made fun of my stutter when I was younger. In my sales job, I got hung up on countless times and to my devastation, one man in the office refused to be on my team due to my stuttering. The shame I felt for being financially wiped out by a man in Central America whom I considered family was devastating.

Except for my peers making fun of me, I never would have imagined any of these things would have happened. All these experiences were way past my worst-case scenario. These circumstances either stunted my confidence or flat-out leveled it. But if I were given the option to erase these experiences from my memory, despite many of them feeling unsurmountable at the time, I'd say no way.

These experiences hurt. But what made them hurt a little less was choosing to show up the next day. In school, being made fun of led me to make friends with people who didn't stand for that nonsense. At work, even though one man refused to be on my team, the rest of the members stayed and we committed to help each other rise together. Once I got my bearings after being crushed in Costa Rica, I took another shot and that path sent me on a journey where I discovered my calling as a writer and coach, and more importantly, it led me to my wife. These experiences taught me loads about not only the longevity of life, but what I'm capable of overcoming, and ultimately, achieving.

Write down both the good, the bad, and the flat-out ugly things that can happen when struggling to bet on yourself. Then pin your ideal outcome on your office wall before setting fire to the others. Remind yourself that going after what we want or doing what we feel is right are the moments when we're living our truth. Maybe things don't immediately turn out as you initially envisioned them. But maybe they do. Maybe they send you on a path you never deemed possible, like waking up each day and making a decent living as a communication consultant and coach who stutters.

It's Our Scars That Make Us Beautiful

I'll always carry with me the story of the woman and the four Christmas cards. But how I learned about it hides another story that I cherish even more. At the time my dad met the elderly couple, he was seventy-three years old. He'd recently retired. Rather than kick back with a Corona and lounging on his La-Z-Boy, before his last day at work, he was already planning and training for his next adventure: walking the Camino de Santiago.

But instead of heading straight to the starting point of the Camino as his start date approached, he flew to Barcelona to visit my wife and me while getting over his jetlag. To this day, in vivid detail, I still remember the exchange we had the morning I walked him to the train station to begin his adventure. This is because, in one action, he demonstrated to me what it takes to squeeze the most out of life.

Despite his ever-present quiet confidence, on this day, I could sense his nerves. "You alright?" I asked. "Yup," he replied as his eyes remained forward. But as soon as the train arrived to take him north, my dad grabbed my shoulder, looked me dead in the eyes, and said—"This is the most scared I've ever been." Then in one fluid motion, he hugged me, grabbed his bag, and made his way onto the train without once looking back.

I stood there paralyzed as early morning commuters rushed past me. "The most scared I've ever been?" I said to myself. "How could this be?" Despite being forty-four years old at the time of writing this book, I still see my dad as a superhero, the kind of guy who's six-foot-five when you close your eyes but five-eleven when you open them. Throughout his career in the military, he learned how to make brave his baseline, navigating hot zones during some of the world's most trying times. Between that and all the twists and turns life filled with love and loss had brought his way, I struggled to make sense of what was so scary about walking across Spain.

But the longer I stood on the platform, the more my eyes began to open to the challenge he was facing. Retiring on its own has to be terrifying. Some people look forward to it. People like my dad, however, have zero interest in moving to Florida. His trip to the Camino marked the beginning of a new chapter. No friends were waiting. He didn't speak the language. Nor did he have any reservations. A seventy-three-year-old American making his way through a foreign country with a backpack and a tent.

Though I was confused when it happened, the image of my dad walking onto the train is one of my most prized memories.

I love the idea that to confidently take his next life steps, he chose to get lost.

I love the idea that no matter how scared he was, turning back was not an option.

I love the fact that choosing to come to Spain and get on that train was his quiet way of shouting—"I'm just getting started."

His time on the Camino was far from perfect. It rained for days on end. He twisted his ankle alone while climbing a foreign mountain. He made wrong turns that led to places that didn't show up on the map. All those imperfections he experienced, however, are his favorite stories today.

Stories like his chance encounter with an elderly couple when he sat down at a bar and said hello in an attempt to make friends.

Stories that teach you the beauty of bruises.

Stories that you only learn by developing the "be bold in the moments that matter" mindset.

Or as my dad might say,

"Stories when we put our fears aside and we got on the damn train anyway!"

PRINCIPLE 12

Lift as You Climb

I STOOD UP FROM THE TABLE, THANKED THE MAN FOR HIS TIME, walked out of the cafe, and proceeded to ask the first person I came across on the street to give me a swift kick in the ass.

When it comes to connecting with people you admire, I'd just committed two cardinal sins. First, in my haste to help myself, I hadn't identified how I could help the man in front of me as much as he could help me. Second, I was asking him for advice on how to do what he does when I hadn't yet put in the work.

In our shared adopted town of Barcelona, the man had an amazing reputation as a coach and creator, the two spaces I wanted to be in. Serial entrepreneur. Leadership and communication senior lecturer at IESE, consistently ranked as the number one school for executive training in the world per the *Financial Times*. Six-figure YouTube audience through the power of educational and entertaining stories. Bylines in mainstream publications. Most of all, people loved him.

As for me, I was fighting to find my footing in my career. I'd moved to Barcelona a few years prior in an attempt to find my smile after losing everything I had in a real estate deal gone wrong in Central America. My experience in the mortgage and real estate industry didn't mean much in Spain. I was moving forward, but it was slow moving. I had my wife. We had our first child. I'd recently discovered a deep love for writing, but I hadn't yet begun to make the impact I was looking to make. I was hoping the conversation with that man would change that. I was hoping he'd be my break.

But that didn't happen.

At least, not the way I saw it playing out.

Forgetting to bring my wallet and making the man float the bill was the least of the mistakes I made that day. At one point, in my jumbled state, I questioned how he could stand living with his partner when he shared a harmless story. When I got home afterward, my wife asked how it went. "I don't think I'll be hearing from him again," I pouted as my newborn son laughed on my lap. "I wasn't ready to meet with him. He knew it. I knew it. I acted like an idiot."

To my surprise, however, a few months later when I began publishing on a make-shift blog I'd made, a comment appeared on the first post. "This is good," it read, "Keep at it." A few months later, when I found the courage to publish another article, it happened again. Only this time, the message read, "This is great!"

It turned out that the very man who made me question my confidence was the very person building it back up again. Shortly thereafter, he was kind enough to offer some thoughts on an article that helped to get it published in *Fast Company*, which ultimately expedited my coaching and writing career.

I've been fortunate to have a lot of good people in my life. My wife. My kids. My parents. My brothers. My friends. My clients. My students. The names of the people you've read in this book. But at the age of thirty-eight, as I was gaining clarity on how to best move forward in my career, few people have had more of an impact than that man, Conor Neill.

A year or so after our first meeting and a handful of emails, Conor and I met again. I did better that time. I felt like I was adding just as much value to him as he was to me. Toward the end of the conversation, I had to know why a sought-after guy like himself would take the time to stick with me. I'll never forget his reply.

In typical Ted Lasso and Conor Neill fashion, it came in the form of a story. "When I was at a crossroads," he began, "a mentor of mine told me that to make an impact, people need to get clear on three things. First, they need clarity in their mission. Second, they need confidence in their actions. Third, and most importantly, they need to have a strong hold on their values." He continued, "I could tell you were lost about the first two parts of this equation. But it was clear we had common values. And when you meet someone like that—someone with shared values—they're worth being given a second, tenth, or even thousandth chance."

It's hard to explain when someone who doesn't have to do something does something. But you feel it a lot. It's also hard not to feel like you're the only person who doesn't have your life together with the never-ending social media loop presenting perfectly packaged people. And maybe some of these people lead lives that are as good as they look. But whether I'm working with recent college grads, business professionals pursuing their master's, creatives, or CEOs, that most mortals don't.

At the time, I'd had some success in my career, but I was experiencing a low. I'd just started a family a few years after being financially wiped out. I was trying to figure out how to create a meaningful career in a new country. I was petrified I wouldn't make ends meet. And here Conor was taking a chance on me. He saw me for my character and not my mistakes. He saw potential and promise when others didn't—when I didn't see that in myself.

Conor's words absolutely leveled me in the best kind of way, while simultaneously his follow-up actions lifted me. Over the years, he's taught me many lessons about being a good person and living a meaningful life. But none is more important than choosing to be the type of person who lifts as you climb.

BE THE PERSON WHO LOOKS BEHIND

Most of us want to connect with people further along in their journey than we are. To get to know people in high places. To even have a few of them as mentors. And this is by no means an attempt to persuade you to not seek out these opportunities and relationships. Getting to know people operating at a higher level is a solid way to level up yourself. I never would have learned this lesson if I hadn't reached out to Conor.

But you don't need to be society's view of an influencer to be influential. And you don't need to be in a society's definition of a position of power for your words to be powerful.

Keep your eyes open to the potential around you.

To those who show promise.

To those who are trying.

If you see potential in someone, why not leave a supportive comment saying to keep at it? If you come across someone who shows promise and you're even an inch further along in the journey, why not reach out to trade ideas? If you see someone trying but struggling in an area you have experience in, why not see if they'd be up to getting on a call to learn more about how your two stories could potentially collide?

We're talking about minimal time investments. Two-minute messages here. Thirty-minute phone calls there. You may find that the words you say and the actions you display impact them the same way Conor's did for me.

That's the beauty of words.

That's their power.

You never know where they may take someone.

Leave a thoughtful comment. Send a much-needed message. Take a moment to see if the new person in the office wants to grab breakfast. Maybe these instances don't result in much. But maybe they do. Maybe they even serve as the tipping point for someone to go all in. Maybe when asked about the people that built them up, they think of you and they say your name.

Many people say the best way to make a name for yourself is by looking at where other people are headed and making a commitment to do the opposite. As more and more people look ahead and prioritize their own goals and to-do lists or have their heads glued to their phones, be the person who chooses to look where others don't.

See the potential around you.

Do what you can to help advance the stories of others.

If you want to be influential, commit to caring for the person standing in front of you.

Choose to Be the Person Who Carries an Extra Blanket

Through Conor's influence, turning this mantra into an operating principle has done more for my career than any other. When I began to get some traction as a writer, I led with this advice in mind, and for every article I published, I edited at least two others for not only friends but people I saw potential in despite not knowing the "rules" for editing.

Sure, it took time, and getting involved for free bit into my short-term earnings when my growing family could have used the money. But it sped up my learning curve tremendously. Over time, the universe paid me back tenfold with friendships and opportunities that stemmed from building a reputation as a fixer and story-bringer-outer of others, roles I never imagined myself having the ability to step into, let alone feel like I comfortably own. I'm proud to have played a lead role in helping people whose messages I strongly believe in to write their books. I'm excited we live in a world where people in positions of power ask someone who writes about his experiences with stuttering to teach leadership and communication at a high level. I'm also thrilled to now operate in the social impact lane and work with people doing a lot of good in the world. But none of those opportunities would have been possible if I hadn't committed to get involved and volunteer in a space that meant a great deal to me.

Out of all the people I've met, however, there's one person and project that stands out and holds a special place in my heart. After doing an interview with my friend Zulie Rane on her popular YouTube channel regarding how to grow an audience as a creator, she forwarded me a nice comment a young writer had left. The message stated he'd read everything I've written and hopes to one day write as well as I do.

That afternoon, I looked up the name George Blue Kelly. And I'm sure glad I did. At the time, my kids were attending a predominantly African school and I'd spoken with a few parents who, like George, traveled to a port in Northern Africa from their respective countries to take rafts to Europe in search of a better life. However, due to the language barrier, in many of the cases, I couldn't dig as deep as I would have liked to learn more about their experiences.

Through George's story, I immediately saw their story. His use of imagery as he stood frozen on the warm shores of Libya with one foot in the boat and one foot cemented to the land under him drew me in. The panic. The doubt. The straight-up fear he and so many others felt. Ultimately, he decided to risk his life in an attempt to make something of himself in a foreign land after losing both his father and brother.

Upon reading his words, I did what people like Kevin Kelley, Fred Dust, Kim Dabbs, Denise Young Smith, Niklas Geoke, Jeanette Bronée, Conor Neill, and so many other good people have done for me and I acted on George's potential. All it took was hearing George's soft, thoughtful voice contrasted with his loud, booming laugh to know we'd be lifelong friends. George lacked vision and clarity, but we shared common values, and thanks to Conor's wisdom, I hit pause to dig deeper when learning about George. He's about as good a person as they get. We immediately decided to collaborate on an article about the lessons he learned since stepping foot on that raft: a decision that many Africans refer to as "The Journey."

If there was one article I'd want the world to read, this would be it. It's not perfect. But it's real. And it's raw. It defines the human experience and the internal struggles we go through in an attempt to find ourselves and to ultimately be someone who matters. There was one particular lesson George shared that perfectly demonstrates the mindset of being someone who lifts as they climb.

While making his way from Nigeria to Libya, George, and his friend he left home with, Eddie, teamed up with another young man and three young women who were barely twenty years of age. This courageous group of six with dreams of Europe clung to each other like family, and over time they became a family as throughout the experience they leaned on each other, drew hope from each other, and gained courage from one another.

As you can imagine, crossing the Sahara is not a fun place to be. When we think of people traveling to Europe on rafts, we see the pictures of the sea and all the lost dreams and stories it holds. But George told me that the desert is the real killer, housing more unmarked graves than the Mediterranean Sea. But it's not just riding in the back of a jam-packed Toyota Helix that has the propensity to flip over while climbing sand mountains the size of Everest. Nor is it only the thieves, rapists, and murderers roaming around looking to take advantage of vulnerable people. But it's also the weather. George is Nigerian. He's used to the heat. But the Sahara was another level, and to match the heat, as soon as the sun went down, the air became bone-chilling cold.

On their first night together, the men noticed the young women sleeping outside under the open sky. "You can't do that!" they warned. "You'll freeze to death." To make matters worse, one of the girls wasn't carrying a blanket. But Paul, the third male wheel on their journey, had brought an extra one and given it to her.

George told me that he sometimes envisions Paul packing for the journey back home while thinking to himself that even though it would take up space, someone may need an extra blanket to keep warm.

I love the image of that and I love that George found inspiration in that visual.

Everyone in this story, from Zulie taking time out of her day to give me a boost by sharing George's message, to George himself, Eddie, Paul, and the three young women that made up their family represent the type of people who look behind. The type of people who realize that what makes all of our journeys memorable is helping each other lift as they climb.

THE MOST IMPACTFUL THOUGHT LEADERS ARE FIRST AND FOREMOST THOUGHTFUL PEOPLE

I've had the privilege to meet, teach, and work with people across the globe and back again. I'm still shy. At times, I still stutter. And don't get me started on the nerves I feel on the first day of class or whenever I have to get on a call or publish an article. But the reason I put myself out into the world is because it's impossible to lead a boring life if you view human beings as endlessly fascinating.

Choose to be in awe of people. Lead with curiosity, not judgment. Take the time to think outside of yourself and keep a running tab on what other people are up to. Choose to lift your head and look behind. Be the type of person who offers a hand when you can to help others achieve more than you ever could. Share what you've learned through your past experiences to help others navigate their present and better design their future.

These decisions and subsequent actions have nothing to do with being outgoing, shy, charismatic, or reserved. Instead, these qualities are a choice every one of us can decide to make. Sure, being obsessive about your own goals may get you to the "destination" faster. But despite what people say, life is long and the things you'll one day hold closest are the people you met along the way. As my friend and author of *Creative Doing*, Herbert Lui said, "Sometimes the best thing you can do is opt to take the 'long cut.'" And there isn't a long cut more valuable and fulfilling than taking the time to support others while opening yourself up to the support of others.

I'm proud of what I've been able to accomplish. I may never be a sought-after speaker, have heads turn when I walk into a room, or say "M-M-Michael began his career selling m-m-mortgages in M-M-Maryland," without tripping up. But I'm cool with that. The life and career I've created today are of my design that's optimized for relationships and doing what I can to use the skills I've honed as a force for good.

But none of it would have been possible if it hadn't been for other people. When you clear the smoke, they're the only thing that matters. The quality of our lives is a direct reflection of the quality of our relationships. This doesn't mean we need to connect with everyone. Sometimes the smallest tribes make the most amount of noise. But it does mean we need to make the effort to be curious about others and learn how to play well with them as two people's vast experiences coming together is the fastest way to make a third.

Life's about committing to learn and listen to the person to your left and your right, in front and behind. It's about taking the time to understand other people's experiences and how they see the world. It's about making the effort to be there for them, developing the courage to allow them to help you, and making the effort to pay it forward whenever and however you can.

Meaningful careers are forged by providing meaningful moments for others. That's also how you become irreplaceable. This comes in many different shapes and sizes. Some take the more vocal approach. But lean into what works for you. Being consistently generous is how you quietly stand out. Wanting the best for others. The most impactful thought leaders are first and foremost thoughtful people.

When I finally realized this, over time, the universe paid me back tenfold by helping reveal my strengths while showing me that my perceived weaknesses were just that—*perceived*. In the process my eyes opened to the fact that my friend Kim Dabbs is absolutely right—the only purpose of finding our power is to share that power with others.

One person at a time.

One conversation at a time.

One story at a time.

The most valuable people take the time to understand what other people value. Learning the stories of others will always be the best way to better write your own.

We don't need to be outgoing or overly vocal to make an impact. We just have to be curious and empathetic and understand thoughtfulness is forever cool.

And if you pay attention and embrace your shy nature, you can do so in as few words as possible.

The Final Word

Care.

ACKNOWLEDGMENTS

A TOKEN OF APPRECIATION

"Remember the good!" That was my mom's wisdom one day when I was going through a rough patch. I've gotten better at implementing her advice over the years. But it took writing this book for me to feel like I've truly cemented the habit. The reason for this is that sitting down for a few hours each day over the last nine months to reflect on my life made me realize just how many people have helped me along the way. From the support of those mentioned in this book to countless others, un abrazo. Looking back, that's what this book is—a collection of people betting on me until I had the courage to believe in myself. I'll never stop paying the generosity forward.

Absolutely none of this would have been possible without my wife, Laia. Shortly after we started our family, I asked her what she thought about me working less and writing more despite barely making rent. Her response: "Yes!" Thank you, Little One. You've given me the greatest gift of all—the permission to wake up each day and be no one other than me. I couldn't be happier that Luc and Liam have you as their life guide and I promise you'll always have a full cup of water on your nightstand.

Speaking of waking up, thank you Luc and Liam for demanding that each day be explored to the twelfth degree. Having the two of you as my early morning rooster screaming "Is it the day yet?" eager to play, has been a godsend. It serves as my constant reminder to get after it and make the stuff I want to see in the world.

A massive hug to my agent Michele Crim for giving me the space to figure things out, and the entire team at Rowman & Littlefield for their guidance and giving me a shot. And of course, my editor, Benjamin Sledge, for working with me from day one, as well as Stephen Moore, Niklas Goeke, Alan Trapulionis, Nova Richards, and Lyuba Golovina for jumping in and carrying me over the line. Endless thanks for turning into a reality the vision of seeing my kids take my story off a bookstore shelf for the first time.

Last, I'd like to thank my mom, dad, and my brothers, Greg and Steve, for helping me navigate life and teaching me perhaps the greatest lesson of all: to never give up on the people you care about.

You're all dream makers.

NOTES

PRINCIPLE 1

1. Vanessa Van Edwards, *Captivate: The Science of Succeeding with People* (Portfolio/Penguin, 2017).

2. Serenity Gibbons, "You and Your Business Have 7 Seconds to Make a First Impression: Here's How to Succeed," *Forbes*, June 19, 2018, https://www.forbes.com/sites/serenitygibbons/2018/06/19/you-have-7-seconds-to-make-a-first-impression-heres-how-to-succeed.

3. Amy Cuddy, "Your Body Language May Shape Who You Are," June 2012 at TEDGlobal, Edinburgh, Scotland, video, https://www.ted.com/talks/amy_cuddy_your_body_language_may_shape_who_you_are.

4. Robin Dreeke, *It's Not All about "Me"* (Robin K. Dreeke, 2011).

PRINCIPLE 2

1. Jack Zenger and Joseph Folkman, "What Great Listeners Actually Do," *Harvard Business Review*, July 14, 2016, https://hbr.org/2016/07/what-great-listeners-actually-do.

PRINCIPLE 3

1. *Ted Lasso*, season 1, episode 8, "The Diamond Dogs," developed by Jason Sudeikis, Bill Lawrence, Brendan Hunt, and Joe Kelly, aired September 18, 2020, on Apple TV.

2. Barry Davret, "How to Judge People Thoughtfully," *Medium*, August 7, 2022, https://barry-davret.medium.com/how-to-judge-people-thoughtfully-c4d701fcc224.

3. Barry Davret, "How to Make Someone Feel Extraordinary by Saying Very Little," *Forge on Medium*, January 2020, https://forge.medium.com/how-to-make-someone-feel-extraordinary-by-saying-very-little-887811246bae.

PRINCIPLE 5

1. Shane Snow, "What We've Learned from Sending 1,000 Cold Emails," *Fast Company*, October 7, 2014, https://www.fastcompany.com/3036672/what-we-learned-from-sending-1000-cold-emails.

PRINCIPLE 6

1. Matthew D. Lieberman, *Social: Why Our Brains Are Wired to Connect* (Crown Publishers, 2013).

2. US Public Health Service, Office of the Surgeon General, *Our Epidemic of Loneliness and Isolation: The U.S. Surgeon General's Advisory on the Healing Effects of Social Connection and Community* (US Department of Health and Human Services, Public Health Service, Office of the Surgeon General, 2023).

3. Sherry Turkle, *Alone Together: Why We Expect More from Technology and Less from Each Other* (Basic Books, 2012).

4. Mike Nizza, "A Simple B.F.F. Strategy, Confirmed by Scientists," *New York Times*, April 8, 2008, https://archive.nytimes.com/thelede.blogs.nytimes.com/2008/04/22/a-simple-bff-strategy-confirmed-by-scientists.

5. Gretchen Rubin, "The More We Talk to Someone, the More We Have to Say," Podcast *Happier*, August 10, 2020, https://gretchenrubin.com/podcast/little-happier-the-more-we-talk-the-more-we-have-to-say/.

PRINCIPLE 7

1. "Dunbar's Number: Why We Can Only Maintain 150 Relationships," BBC, accessed June 1, 2023,
https://www.bbc.com/future/article/20191001-dunbars-number-why-we-can-only-maintain-150-relationships.

2. Jenny Gross, "Can You Have More Than 150 Friends?" *New York Times*, May 11, 2021,
https://www.nytimes.com/2021/05/11/science/dunbars-number-debunked.html.

PRINCIPLE 8

1. Mark S. Granovetter, "The Strength of Weak Ties," *American Journal of Sociology* 78, no. 6 (May 1973).

2. Kathleen Wong, "LinkedIn Ran Undisclosed Social Experiments on 20 Million Users for Years to Study Job Success," *USA Today*, https://eu.usatoday.com/story/money/2022/09/25/linkedin-ran-secret-social-experiments-on-20-million-users/8115007001/.

3. George Anders, "Using 'Weak Ties' to Aid Your Job Hunt: What a Giant Study Can Teach Us," *LinkedIn*, September 15, 2022,

https://www.linkedin.com/pulse/using-weak-ties-aid-your-job-hunt-what
-giant-study-can-george-anders/.

4. Brieanna Nicker, "Echo Chambers, Rabbit Holes, and Ideological Bias: How
YouTube Recommends Content to Real Users," *Brookings Institution*, October
13, 2022, https://www.brookings.edu/articles/echo-chambers-rabbit-holes-and
-ideological-bias-how-youtube-recommends-content-to-real-users/.

PRINCIPLE 9

1. Jonathan Marks, "Word Roots and Routes: Duce, Duct," *Macmillan Dictionary Blog*, 2014, https://www.macmillandictionaryblog.com/word-roots-and
-routes-duce-duct.

2. Colleen De Bellefonds, "Why Michael Phelps Has the Perfect Body for
Swimming," *Biography*, May 14, 2020, https://www.biography.com/athletes/
michael-phelp-perfect-body-swimming

PRINCIPLE 11

1. Jeanette Bronée, *The Self-Care Mindset: Rethinking How We Change and
Grow, Harness Well-Being, and Reclaim Work-Life Quality* (Wiley, 2022).

BIBLIOGRAPHY

Anders, George. "Using 'Weak Ties' to Aid Your Job Hunt: What a Giant Study Can Teach Us." *LinkedIn*, September 15, 2022. https://www.linkedin.com /pulse/using-weak-ties-aid-your-job-hunt-what-giant-study-can-george -anders/.

BBC. "Dunbar's Number: Why We Can Only Maintain 150 Relationships."- Accessed June 1, 2023. https://www.bbc.com/future/article/20191001 -dunbars-number-why-we-can-only-maintain-150-relationships.

Bronée, Jeanette. *The Self-Care Mindset: Rethinking How We Change and Grow, Harness Well-Being, and Reclaim Work-Life Quality.* Wiley, 2022.

Cuddy, Amy. "Your Body Language May Shape Who You Are." Filmed June 2012 at TEDGlobal, Edinburgh, Scotland. Video. https://www.ted.com/ talks/amy_cuddy_your_body_language_may_shape_who_you_are.

Davret, Barry. "How to Judge People Thoughtfully." *Medium*, August 7, 2022. https://barry-davret.medium.com/how-to-judge-people -thoughtfully-c4d701fcc224.

———. "How to Make Someone Feel Extraordinary by Saying Very Little." *Forge on Medium*, January 2020. https://forge.medium.com/how-to-make -someone-feel-extraordinary-by-saying-very-little-887811246bae.

De Bellefonds, Colleen. "Why Michael Phelps Has the Perfect Body for Swimming." *Biography*, May 14, 2020. https://www.biography.com/athletes/ michael-phelp-perfect-body-swimming.

Dreeke, Robin. *It's Not All about "Me."* Robin K. Dreeke, 2011.

Gibbons, Serenity. "You and Your Business Have 7 Seconds to Make a First Impression: Here's How to Succeed." *Forbes*, June 19, 2018. https://www .forbes.com/sites/serenitygibbons/2018/06/19/you-have-7-seconds-to -make-a-first-impression-heres-how-to-succeed.

Granovetter, Mark S. "The Strength of Weak Ties." *American Journal of Sociology* 78, no. 6 (May 1973).

Gross, Jenny. "Can You Have More Than 150 Friends?" *New York Times*, May 11, 2021. https://www.nytimes.com/2021/05/11/science/dunbars-number -debunked.html.

Lieberman, Matthew D. *Social: Why Our Brains Are Wired to Connect*. Crown Publishers, 2013.

Marks, Jonathan. "Word Roots and Routes: Duce, Duct." *Macmillan Dictionary Blog*, 2014. https://www.macmillandictionaryblog.com/word-roots-and-routes-duce-duct

Nicker, Brieanna. "Echo Chambers, Rabbit Holes, and Ideological Bias: How YouTube Recommends Content to Real Users." *Brookings Institution*, October 13, 2022. https://www.brookings.edu/articles/echo-chambers-rabbit-holes-and-ideological-bias-how-youtube-recommends-content-to-real-users/.

Nizza, Mike. "A Simple B.F.F. Strategy, Confirmed by Scientists." *New York Times*, April 8, 2008. https://archive.nytimes.com/thelede.blogs.nytimes.com/2008/04/22/a-simple-bff-strategy-confirmed-by-scientists.

US Public Health Service. Office of the Surgeon General. *Our Epidemic of Loneliness and Isolation: The U.S. Surgeon General's Advisory on the Healing Effects of Social Connection and Community*. US Department of Health and Human Services, Public Health Service, Office of the Surgeon General, 2023. https://www.hhs.gov/sites/default/files/surgeon-general-social-connection-advisory.pdf.

Rubin, Gretchen. "The More We Talk to Someone, the More We Have to Say." Podcast Happier, August 10, 2020. https://gretchenrubin.com/podcast/little-happier-the-more-we-talk-the-more-we-have-to-say/.

Snow, Shane. "What We've Learned From Sending 1,000 Cold Emails." *Fast Company*, October 7, 2014. https://www.fastcompany.com/3036672/what-we-learned-from-sending-1000-cold-emails.

Sudeikis, Jason, Bill Lawrence, Brendan Hunt, and Joe Kelly, developers. *Ted Lasso*. Season 1, episode 8, "The Diamond Dogs." Aired September 18, 2020, on Apple TV.

Turkle, Sherry. *Alone Together: Why We Expect More from Technology and Less from Each Other*. New York: Basic Books, 2012.

Van Edwards, Vanessa. *Captivate: The Science of Succeeding with People*. Portfolio/Penguin, 2017.

Wong, Kathleen. "LinkedIn Ran Undisclosed Social Experiments on 20 Million Users for Years to Study Job Success." *USA Today*, September 25, 2022. https://eu.usatoday.com/story/money/2022/09/25/linkedin-ran-secret-social-experiments-on-20-million-users/8115007001/.

Zenger, Jack, and Joseph Folkman. "What Great Listeners Actually Do." *Harvard Business Review*, July 14, 2016. https://hbr.org/2016/07/what-great-listeners-actually-do.

Index

AAA framework
(Acknowledge, Accept,
Ask), 163–65
acting through fear, 161–
63, 168
active listening, 22
act of service, leadership as,
130–31
admired people, connections
with, 171–72
algorithms, 115, 119
*American Journal of
Sociology*, 112
Anders, George, 114, 119–20
Anthony (friend): loneliness,
4; maintaining relationships,
81–83, 93–94; and note-
taking, 88anxiety: public
speaking, 45–47; from work
stress, 93, 98, 129
asking: for help, 165;
questions, 44; for what you
want, 156–57
authenticity, 72
awe of others, 57–58

Barcelona, Spain, 75–76, 84,
146–47, 159, 171–72
"be a biographer," 25–26
"be a feather," 22–24
"be a set designer," 24–25
"be a smart parrot," 27–28
"be a trampoline," 27
Behavioral Analysis Program,
FBI, 16
benefits, from weak ties,
114–15, 117–18
"be the opposite of a
cricket," 29
blogs, 172; connecting
through, 71; *Cup of Jo*,
98, 101; sharing via, 136–
37, 142
body language, 13; in
interviews, 56; during
introductory meeting,
11–12, 155–56
boldness, 155–56, 169;
building muscle of, 163;
collect moments of, 160–62;
leading with, 157–59
Bonus Time (Pennie), 77

bragging, about friends, 92
bravery, 168; boldness as, 160–61; daily steps of, 162–63
Brison, Todd, 26
Bronée, Jeanette, 164–66
Brookings Institution, 115
Brosio, Jon, 136, 137
building confidence: cheat sheet for, 48–51; through outreach, 68–69; personalized messages for, 120–21; writing exercise for, 56
building connections, 58; improvement in, 4, 16; letters for, 64–67; through presence, 21–22, 23; as primary motivator, 48; prioritizing comfort zone when, 86; through questions, 36–37, 44; self-talk and, 10, 19; strategy for, 12–13; technology for, 67–68, 70, 87–89, 119; that last, 92, 148
building networks, 108–9, 122
"Business for Good," 113

Caffrey, Justin, 93
Camino de Santiago, Spain, 155–56, 167–68
Can You Have More than 150 Friends? (Lind), 103
Captivate (Edwards), 9–10

career advice, as conversation starter, 15
career success, 55, 97–98
Challenges, to listening, 23–24
ChatGPT, 116
cheat sheet, for building confidence, 48–51
choices: friendships are, 83–84; power of, 144–45
classroom environment, 24, 43
closed questions, 37
collaboration, 102; partners in, 107–9; with students, 130–31
collecting moments, of boldness, 160–62
comfort, 11–12
comfort zone, in building connections, 86
commitment: to listen, 17; to showing up, 161–62, 166–67
communication: consistency in, 121–22; follow-ups in, 87, 91; frequency in, 89–90; lines of, 85; nonverbal, 20; with strangers, 46; verbal, 20
communication skills, 46–47, 49–50, 51–52, 56
community, 42; connections in, 12–13; success due to, 98
complimentary skills, 106–7, 108

confidence, 11–12, 45, 62; building, 48–51, 56, 68–69, 121; destroyed, 23; quiet, 7–8; sharing stories with, 146

conflict, due to stutter, 125–27

connections: through blog, 71; common, 72; community, 12–13; impact of, 172–73; invitation for, 138; on LinkedIn, 71, 100–101; online, 74–76, 86–88, 100–102; with people you admire, 171–72; quality of, 104, 179; through similar interests, 117–18; through X, 119. *See also* building connections

Connors, Christopher, 86–87, 91

contacting professionals, 118–19, 121–22; in your field, 63–68, 78–79

conventional wisdom, 77–78

conversation personas, 22–23

conversations: listening during, 17, 19–22; summarizing, 28; tone in, 38

conversation starters, 15

corporate trainer, 127; experience with, 3–6; influence from, 16–17, 88

Corrigan, Kelly, 54–55, 57

courage, in sales job, 47, 138

COVID-19, 76, 164

The Creative Act (Rubin, R.), 144

Creative Doing (Lui), 179

Cup of Jo (blog), 98, 101

curiosity: importance of, 112; listening as, 21; about others, 179–80; as primary responsibility, 32–36, 38, 40, 44, 58, 63; sharing stories with, 42; spark of, 14, 20; with speech therapy, 19

Dabbs, Kim, 14, 107, 180

daily prompts, 50

daily steps, of bravery, 162–63

Davret, Barry, 34, 38

decisions, life-changing, 98–99

defense mechanism, 81

defining relationships, 149

defining values, 149–51

definition, of a story, 143

design, 10; environment, 24–25, 29; life timeline, 148–51

details, importance of, 76, 88–89

direct messages, on LinkedIn, 77

dissecting: before speaking, 52–54; your past, 145–47

diverse perspectives, 116–17, 118

diversity, in relationships: importance of, 118–20; through weak ties, 110, 122

Drake, 136

Dreeke, Robin, 16

Dunbar, Robin, 103–4

Dunbar's number, 103–4

Dust, Fred, 113–14

Eames, Charles, 76

echo chamber, 115, 117

effectiveness, in sharing stories, 137–38

effective teachers, 132–33

"effortfulness," 94

ego: putting aside our, 21; of Smith, 36; Ted Lasso and, 33, 39

email, 35

Emotional Intelligence for the Modern Leader (Connors), 86, 91

empathy, 21

environment, classroom, 24, 43

environment design, 24–25, 29

evaluation, of candidates, 106

experts, types of, 132–33

exploration questions, 36–38

Fast Company, 172

fear: acting through, 161–63, 168; human condition and, 160; of rejection, 85, 157; of sending messages, 66–67

Ferriss, Tim, 132

Financial Times, 171

Folkman, Joseph, 27

follow-ups, in communication, 87–88, 91

Foroux, Darius, 57

framework, AAA, 163–65

friends: bragging about, 92; heroes into, 67–68; making, 81; quarantine helping identify, 105; on social media, 89

friendships, are choices, 83–84

future, writing your, 145–48

generosity, vulnerability as, 126–28

goals, as north star, 70

Goddard, Joanna, 98

Godin, Seth, 99, 109

Goeke, Niklas, 98–100, 109

Granovetter, Mark, 112–13

Grigoryev, Alex (student), 91–92

Günel, Sinem, guidance from, 135, 136, 137

Happier (podcast), 90

The Happiness Project (Rubin, G.), 90

Harvard Business Review, 27

Harvard University, 61–63, 65

hashtags, social media, 101
help: asking for, 165; for professionals, 73–75
heroes, 63, 67–68
hobbies, 14, 26
honesty, 143–45
How I Built This (podcast), 102
human behavior principles, 62
human condition: fear and, 160; judgement and, 33; loneliness and, 90
humanization, 73

ice-breakers, 14–15
ideas, sharing for free, 91–92
idea sex, 116
identity, journey to, 141–43
IESE (Barcelona), 171
impact, of connections, 172–73
imperfections, 3, 8
impressions, stand-out, 75–76
improvement, in building connections, 4, 16
inadequacy, 141–42
indirect outreach, 70–71
individual strengths, 134–35
influencer, 92, 174–75
insecurities: fatherhood related, 139–42; masking, 81
intellectually alive, 112
intellectually dead, 111–12, 116
intentionality, 87, 88–89

internal chatter, 8–9, 19, 23–24, 140
internal dialog, 10, 54
internal narrative, 8
interviews: body language in, 56; job, 46, 48; preparation for, 55–56; questions for, 49–50
interview skills, 49
introductory meetings: body language during, 11–12, 155–56; guiding, 25–26; ice-breakers used in, 14–15; variety of, 13
invitation, for connections, 138
Irreplaceable (Kelley), 61
It's Not All About "Me" (Dreeke), 16

job interviews, 46, 48
joining online groups, 108–9
journey, to identity, 141–43
judgment: closed questions and, 37; human condition and, 33; letting go of, 42; losing from, 40–41; Smith and, 35–36; as survival, 34; Ted Lasso and, 32–33; work team and, 129

Kelley, Kevin: advice from, 57–58, 67; background of, 61–66; candidate evaluation strategy of, 106–7; on effortfulness, 94–95; learning from, 69; on rejection, 78

Kelly, George Blue, 176–78

Kelly Corrigan Wonders (podcast), 54

Kent, Roy (fictional character), 39–40

Mr. Kitchen (teacher), 51

knowledge, sharing of, 132–36

Kohn, Gene, 61–63, 69

Laia (wife), 97, 151; first meeting, 159–60; on prioritizing relationships, 105; starting a family with, 139–41

Lasso, Ted (fictional character), 44; ego and, 33, 39; judgement and, 32–33; philosophy of, 31–33; storytelling with, 173; vulnerability of, 39–40

lasting connections, 92, 148

leaders, 6; linguistics of, 131; thought, 178–80; variety of, 130

leadership, 33; act of service as, 130–31; communication lecturer and, 43; teaching as, 129–31, 133–34; types of, 126–27, 130–31

leading with boldness, 157–59

The Legend of Bagger Vance (Pressfield), 71

letters, for building connections, 64–67, 157

letting go, of judgement, 42

Liam (son), 140–41, 151

Lieberman, Matthew D., 83

life: experiences, 166–69; meaningful things in, 160; patterns in, 166; reflection on, 149–50

life-changing decisions, 98–99

life timeline, designing, 148–51

"lift as you climb," 173, 177–78

like-minded people, 69

Lind, Johan, 103–4

linguistics, of leaders, 131

LinkedIn, 119, 136; connecting on, 71, 100–101; direct messages on, 77; friends on, 89; managing weak ties and, 120; relationship study by, 114, 118; students on, 41

listening, 7, 10; active, 22; challenges to, 23–24; commitment to, 17; during conversations, 17, 19–22; curiosity as, 21; reflective, 28–29

loneliness: Anthony and, 84; as part of human condition,

90; rates of, 83; working through, 84

long-term relationships, 82–83

Luc (son), 97, 151

Lui, Herbert, 179

magnet, sharing as, 136–38

maintaining relationships: Anthony on, 81–83, 93–94; intentionality in, 87–89; messaging for, 85–86

Making Conversation (Dust), 113

management, of weak ties, 119–22

management team, 7

manager support, for perceived weakness, 17

marketing tactics, 143

masking: insecurities, 81; as survival mechanism, 23

mastermind group: engagement in, 102; forming, 99; operating principles for, 100–1

meaningful things, in life, 160

Medium, 34; engaging audiences in, 57; followers on, 66; sharing via, 136

meetups, 94–95

mentorship, 78, 135, 136, 173, 174

messages, personalized, 120–21

Mihaj, Alba (student), 147

Moore, Stephen (friend), 107, 165

mortgage business, 3, 5, 171, 179

The Moth, 53

motivator, primary, 48, 148

Murthy, Vivek, 83

muscle of boldness, 163

Nait, Martin, 77

name-dropper, 92–93

negative internal dialog, 54

Neill, Conor, 172–73, 174, 175, 177

networks, 69; building, 108–9, 122; patchwork, 105–7; sharing, 93; supportive, 103–4

New York Times, 89, 103

nonverbal communication, 20

north star, goals as, 70

note-taking, 151; Anthony on, 88; interview exercise with, 50; listening exercise with, 19–20, 26; observation with, 51; recording exercise with, 56

observations: making friends and, 81; before speaking, 51–52

Okumora, Kaki, 66

"one plus one equals three," 117
online connections: effective outreach for, 74–76; following up with, 87–88; prioritizing comfort zone with, 86; through Slack, 99–102, 108
online groups: joining, 108–9; operating principles for, 100–101
open-ended questions, 37
Oprah Magazine, 71
others: awe of, 57–58; curiosity about, 179–80; stories of, 25–26, 38–41, 64, 175, 180
outreach: building confidence through, 68–69; indirect, 70–71, limited, 68, for online connections, 74–76
outreach message, 70, 72; draft for, 74–75; sample format for, 73
owning your story, 139, 150

Palmer, Anne, 113–14
Pang, May, 26
panic attacks, 4–5
parenting, 111
partners, in collaboration, 107–9
past, dissecting your, 145–47
patchwork networks, 105–7
patterns, in life, 166

Pennie, Brian, 77
people-pleaser, 164
perceived weakness: manager support for, 17; overcoming, 180; questioning, 8–9; stutter as, 10, 19, 34, 35
personalized messages, 120–21
personal stories, power of, 116
personas, in conversation, 22–23
perspectives, diverse, 116–17, 118
Phelps, Michael, 132–33
philosophy, of Ted Lasso, 31–33
podcasts, 53–55; *Happier*, 90; *How I Built This*, 102; *Kelly Corrigan Wonders*, 54
potential, 158, supporting others with, 174–75, 176–77, 179–80
power: of choices, 144–45; of personalized stories, 116; of quirks, 76; of weak ties, 112–13, 116; of who, 78–79; of words, 174–75
preparation, for interview, 55–56
presence, building connections through, 21–22, 23
presentations, 45–48, 55–56, 72; giving, 131, 136–37, 159, 161; observing, 51; preparing for, 50, 165

Pressfield, Steven, 71
primary motivator, 148;
    building connections as, 48
primary responsibility,
    curiosity as, 32–36, 38, 40,
    44, 58, 63
principles of human
    behavior, 62
prioritize relationships, 89,
    93–95, 105
problem solving, 7, 28, 50
professionals: contacting,
    63–68, 78–79, 118–19,
    121–22; help for, 73–75;
    positive impact from, 72
progress, 108, 128
prompts, daily, 38, 50
psychological safety, 25
public speaking, 48; anxiety
    from, 45–47; daily
    steps of bravery in, 163;
    stutter during, 46–47

quality, of connections,
    104, 179
quarantine: communication
    during, 90; identifying
    friends during, 105
questions: asking, 44; building
    connections through, 36–37,
    44; closed, 37; exploration,
    36–38; interview, 49–50;
    open-ended, 37

quick messages, types of,
    120–22
quiet confidence, 7–8, 167–68
quietness, 9
quirks, power of, 76
#quoteyourconnections, 101

Rane, Zulie, 176
rates of loneliness, 83
Raz, Guy, 102
record yourself talking, 54–56
recurring meetups, 94–95
referrals, 134–35, 137
reflection, 149–50
reflective listening, 27–28
regrets, as reminders, 157–58
rejection, fear of, 85, 157
relationships: defining, 149;
    diversity in, 110, 118–20,
    122; helping Shook Kelley,
    64–65; long-term, 82–83;
    maintaining, 81–83, 85–87,
    89, 93–94; prioritize, 89,
    93–95
relationship study, LinkedIn,
    114, 118
"remember the good," 46–47
reputation, 39, 66, 93, 135,
    136, 171, 175
research, 26, 76; conducting,
    64; sharing, 132; through
    social media, 73
retirement, 3–4, 111–12
role play, 4–5, 16

Rubin, Gretchen, 90
Rubin, Rick, 144–45
"Rule of 7," 70–71, 85–86

safety: in environment, 43, 147; psychological, 25
sales call, 5
sales job, 127; of Anthony, 82; courage in taking, 47, 138; daily steps of bravery at, 162; experience through, 88
sales manager, 125–30, 134
sales rep, 3–4, 7–8
sample format, for outreach message, 73
Sarandeses, Rafa, 21
scars, as beautiful, 167–69
scenarios, worst-case, 166–67
Schaefer, Warren, 29
self: qualities of, 141–42; underestimate, 73–75
self-awareness, 50
self-care, 164–65
The Self-Care Mindset (Bronée), 164–65
self-expression, 47–48, 58, 144
self-help, 11, 91
self-improvement, technology for, 57
self-talk: building connections and, 10, 19; transformation, 6, 166
self-validation, 161
self-worth, 151–52

sending messages, fear of, 66–67
set designer advice, 24–25
shame, in internal chatter, 140
shared values, 173
sharing: experiences, 117; ideas for free, 91–92; insecurities, 142; knowledge, 132–36; networks, 93
sharing stories, 41–44, 143–44, 148; with confidence, 146; with curiosity, 179–80; effectiveness of, 137–38; with vulnerability, 147
Shearn, Amy, 71
Shook Kelley (design firm), 61, 64–65, 106
showing up, commitment to, 161–62, 166–67
shyness. *See specific topics*
silence, 29
similar interests, making connections through, 117–18
Sinek, Simon, 31
skills: in communication, 46–47, 49–50, 51–52, 56; complimentary, 106–7, 108; interview, 49; variety in, 134–35; writing, 65
Slack (productivity platform): making groups in, 99; meeting others through, 100–102, 108

Sledge, Benjamin, 78

"slow is smooth and smooth is fast," 84–85

small groups, 102–3, 109

small talk: bypassing, 148; examples of, 14–15; making others feel comfortable with, 85; reaching goals through, 163; as secret weapon, 13

smart parrot advice, 27–28

Smith, Denise Young: advice from, 28, 37; connecting with, 35–36; ego of, 36; judgement and, 35–36

Snow, Shane, 72

social media: focusing on one person from, 68; friends, 89; hashtags, 101; research through, 73

Social: Why Our Brains Are Wired to Connect (Lieberman), 83

spark of curiosity, 14, 20

speaker tactics, 52–54

speech introductions, 52, 56

speech therapist, 46; advice from, 19–20, 51

speech transitions, 52

spontaneous trait inferences (STI), 92

standing up, for yourself, 161

stand-out impressions, 75–76

starting a family, 139–41

Start with Why (Sinek), 31

stories: definition of, 143; of others, 25–26, 38–41, 64, 175, 180; owning your, 139, 150; sharing, 41–44, 137–38, 143–44, 146–48, 179–80; of struggle, 53; student, 42–44

storytelling, 143–45, 173

story-worthy, 146, 150

strangers, communication with, 46

strategy, for building connections, 12–13

"The Strength of Weak Ties" (Granovetter), 112

strengths: enthusiasm as, 67; individual, 134–35; stutter as, 129; of vulnerability, 39–40; in weak ties, 112–13, 114, 119–20, 122

students: collaboration with, 130–31; on LinkedIn, 41

student stories, 42–44

stutter, 41–42; conflict due to, 125–27; growing up with, 81; perceived weakness as, 8–9, 10, 19, 34, 35; during public speaking, 46–47; as strength, 129; working with, 4–5, 6–7

subject line, outreach message, 71–72

success: career, 55, 97–98; community helping with, 98
support: for others with potential, 174–75, 176–77, 179–80; team, 128–29; for weaknesses, 128
supportive networks, 103–4
survival, judgement as, 34
survival mechanism: determining threats as, 15–16; laughing as, 125; masking as, 23

tactics: in marketing, 143; speaker, 52–54
taking action, 157–60
Tartt, Jamie (fictional character), 39–40
teachers, effective, 132–33
teaching, as leadership, 129–31; potential for, 133–34
team support, 128–29
technology: building connections with, 67–68, 70, 87–89, 119; knowledge, 135–36; for self-improvement, 57
Ted Lasso, 31–32, 33, 39–40, 44, 173
TED Talk, 53, 135
Tell Me More (PBS show), 54
Thatcher, Margaret, 45

thoughtfulness, 16–17, 178–80; displaying, 71; reputation of, 66
thought leaders, 178–80
tone, in conversations, 38
topics, of conversation, 26
trainer, corporate, 3–6, 16–17, 88, 127
trampoline advice, 27
transformation, of self-talk, 6, 166
transition statements, 38
true self, 10
Turkle, Sherry, 84

underestimation of self, 73–75
United Nations, 146
Unseen City (Shearn), 71

valuable people, 10, 20, 180
values: defining, 149–51; shared, 173
Van Edwards, Vanessa, 9–10
verbal communication, 20
vulnerability, 142; generosity as, 126–28; sharing stories with, 147; of Ted Lasso, 39–40

The War of Art (Pressfield), 71
weakness: perceived, 8–10, 17, 19, 34, 35, 180; support for, 128

weak ties, 104–5, 110–11; Anders advice on, 119–20; benefits from, 114–15, 117–18; LinkedIn to manage, 120; managing, 119–22; power of, 112–13, 116

"What Great Listeners Actually Do" (Zenger and Folkman), 27

what you want, asking for, 156–57

Where Cowards Go to Die (Sledge), 78

who, power of, 78–79

Wignall, Nick, 27–29, 101

wisdom, conventional, 77–78

Wolny, Nick, 55

words, power of, 174–75

"Words Matter" (Smith), 35

work: benefitting others, 131–32; difficult tasks at, 129; with stutter, 4–5, 6–7

work stress, anxiety from, 93, 98, 129

work team, 125–28, 129

worst-case scenarios, 166–67

writing: daily steps of bravery in, 162–63; exercise for building confidence, 56; skills, 65; before speaking, 48–51; your future, 145–48

You Belong Here (Dabbs), 14, 107

YouTube, 48; algorithm of, 115; audience, 171; Goeke and, 99; Rane channel on, 176; sharing via, 136

Zenger, Jack, 27

About the Author

Michael Thompson is a career coach, leadership and communication lecturer at EAE Business School in Barcelona, Spain, and a strategic communication advisor to top business leaders around the globe. Growing up, he had a debilitating speech impediment and social anxiety that kept him from pursuing his goals. By fighting to turn his supposed weaknesses into his greatest strengths, he developed a system of principles to help other shy people to more confidently express themselves and build meaningful relationships without sacrificing their quiet nature. He is the author of many viral articles on Medium.com and his work has been featured in dozens of mainstream business and life publications including *Business Insider* and *Fast Company*. *Shy by Design:12 Timeless Principles to Quietly Stand Out* is Michael's debut book. When he's not working with students and clients to get their words to rise, he can be found exploring the Mediterranean with his wife and their two young boys in his adopted home of Palamós, Spain.